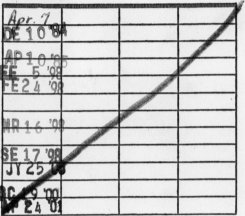

DOGMA, DEPRESSION, AND THE NEW DEAL

THEODORE ROSENOF

DOGMA, DEPRESSION, AND THE NEW DEAL

The Debate of Political Leaders over Economic Recovery

National University Publications
KENNIKAT PRESS • 1975
Port Washington, N.Y. • London

Manufactured in the United States of America

Published by
Kennikat Press Corp.
Port Washington, N.Y. / London

Library of Congress Cataloging in Publication Data

Rosenof, Theodore.
   Dogma, depression, and the New Deal

   (National university publications)
   Includes bibliographical references and index.
   1. United States—Economic policy—1933–1945.
I. Title.
HC106.3.R598   330.9′73′0917   75-15506
ISBN 0-8046-9113-4

CONTENTS

PREFACE

There is a vast body of literature on the New Deal years, much of which treats of biography, episodes, and agencies in a chronological narrative fashion. I have chosen to depart from this familiar narrative approach which tells (or retells or amplifies) the story of some particular individual or episode or agency and to look at one aspect of these years from a different angle. My central objective is to systematize the 1933–38 debate among political leaders over the issue of recovery. I view these political leaders primarily in their roles as public men engaged in public discussion rather than as private individuals; moreover, my interest is more in the ideological patterns of the period than with the ideas of particular men. Research into the latter, however, provides the necessary empirical basis for the determination of the former. The views of specific leaders provide the medium through which the patterns of thought can be distinguished and schematized. I believe that this approach, cutting across biographical, group, and topical lines, can ascertain patterns which might not otherwise be noted.

The views of "political leaders" form the substance of this study. It is necessary to be somewhat arbitrary in applying this group categorization, but I have tried to include those individuals who were significantly active in the political arena. Words such as "progressive," "radical," "New Dealer," and "conservative" also have their limitations and flaws; they, too, are necessarily defined and applied somewhat arbitrarily. Yet they can, in a limited way and for a limited purpose, be useful. This is not to say that such political categories are (or were) rigorously precise. They are not, nor are they my major concern. They are here used primarily for purposes of identification, for an indication of what kinds of political men took what kinds of ideological positions. My primary concern is not with political but with ideological categories; above all, my concern is with the nature of the debate itself, with what its contours and characteristics suggest about the nature of the American ideological tradition.

These terms—progressive, radical, New Dealer, and conservative—are used to characterize men who by and large were so characterized by contemporaries. Moreover, men generally characterized as conservative cohered in stressing what I have labeled the "confidence thesis." Men generally characterized as New Dealer, progressive, and radical generally cohered in stressing what I have called the "purchasing power thesis." There were, to be sure, ideological differences within each camp. Old-line Democratic conservatives differed in some ways with New Era Republican conservatives—on foreign trade policy, for example. Such "modern" progressives as Robert M. La Follette, Jr., and Fiorello La Guardia were more attuned to the spirit of the early New Deal than were William Borah and Burton Wheeler. Progressives, New Dealers, and radicals differed over how to implement the purchasing power thesis, the former groups looking to reformist programs, and the latter going beyond reform to demand a new economic "system." Various political leaders, further, did not fit clearly into any of these categories. Some Democrats, for example, were neither firm New Dealers nor conservatives, and often stressed the need for an expanded export trade as the road to recovery. Others, including men from both parties, were of a neopopulist bent and stressed currency expansion as the depression's remedy.

Various political leaders, no doubt, twisted and turned (at least within certain ideological limits) according to political expediency; others moderated their rhetoric or retreated into relative silence for similar reasons. Yet, while such forces are undeniably operative, their existence does not mean that political expressions of ideas should or can be generally dismissed as expedient rhetoric, geared to political opportunism. While politicians do operate within the context of certain political realities, they also operate within certain ideological bounds. While political considerations were operative in the thirties they seemed to have a relatively marginal effect on ideas, influencing emphases and rhetoric more than substantive attitudes. I have relied upon the mass of printed material available, upon those primary sources—such as books, articles, and speeches—in which systematic ideas would most likely be presented. I have also tried to cast a wide net for secondary accounts which utilized manuscript sources, but such studies seldom added materially to what I was able to glean from other sources. Indeed, most such studies, when dealing with their protagonists' ideas, relied upon the same kinds of sources I have used.

Political leaders may, and no doubt often do, fashion their arguments to meet what they consider to be the needs of economic groups among the electorate, but I do not believe that this should preclude a study which focuses upon ideas as ideas. The detailed task, say, of determining the relationship of senators to economic groups in their states is that of the institutional historian and the biographer; it is a task in itself, and distinct from the one which I have undertaken. My primary concern here is with the nature of the ideas expressed and not with their underlying sources, with the delineation and distillation of the debate, with an analysis of the patterns of American ideology. In dealing with the interrelationships of ideas, and recognizing that there are difficulties involved in determining with empirical precision the genuineness of ideas, I have tried to show how and why in terms of their overall philosophical persuasions men of differing persuasions could arrive at their (sometimes similar) positions on particular problems.

The particular positions of political leaders (and groups) did—when interrelated and schematized—have an ideological-philosophical consistency. Various groups did have overall philosophical assumptions from which their specific stands derived and with which their specific stands cohered. The conservatives, for example, who looked at reforms and readjustments and saw fascism, communism, autocracy, regimentation, and the end of all precious values and freedoms and the American way of life, *did* link these fears and assertions within a consistent philosophical schema. Their cries about the New Deal being the "road" to all sorts of horror must be placed both within the context of the time—the apparent decline in the thirties of western democracy and the rise of cultural, political, and ideological authoritarianism—and the context of their assumptions about the nature of the economy and its relationship to society and government. Similarly, the New Dealers, taken as a group, did have an operative series of ideological assumptions which served both to shape and to limit their policy choices in particular areas. Like *the* New Dealer, Franklin Roosevelt, the New Dealers as a group were pragmatic and experimentalist only within certain ideological bounds; like conservatives and radicals they, too, operated upon the basis of fundamental ideological assumptions about the nature of the economy and its relation to larger social and political phenomena.

The reader will not find here the familiar stories of administrative conflicts among individuals and groups in the New Deal, stories frequently told from numerous viewpoints and perspectives. Thus there will be no retelling of the struggles between Henry Wallace and George Peek, or Hugh Johnson and Donald Richberg, or between Henry Morgenthau, Jr., and the spenders, or Cordell Hull and his detractors, and so on. Nor will the reader once again find sketches of familiar personalities of the era. Rather I have tried to go beyond these familiar phenomena to delineate and analyze basic ideological patterns. This is not to say that such controversies and personalities are unimportant; it is simply to suggest that the literature is replete with them and that other approaches may now be more useful and illuminating.

I have not tried here to take a representative sampling of political leaders, to concentrate upon a "representative" New Dealer, progressive, radical, and conservative, or upon "representative" exponents of the various recovery theses. Such a sampling would not be without its uses, but it is obviously less valid empirically than a fuller examination. Therefore I have tried to examine the views of all those who were nationally prominent political leaders during the period. This required the perusal of much repetitive material, but it also provided a surer empirical base than a limited sampling. In the text, of course, the examples of given positions must necessarily be limited, but notes provide further examples, and generalizations are based upon detailed evidence.

Generalizations about individuals' positions are based upon statements consistently made before various groups, under various circumstances, and at various times. Proponents of the purchasing power thesis, the confidence thesis, the money cure, and the exports cure, for example, repeated their positions in context after context, before group after group, and time after time. Where there were changes or ambiguities I have exposited and tried to explain them. But the point to be made and stressed is that basic positions were expressed so frequently and under such a variety of circumstances that their genuineness may be assumed apart from any particular occasion or context. Most importantly, given the large empirical base of this study, generalizations about group positions are based upon consistent and repeated expressions of opinion by many individuals under many circumstances and in many contexts. Thus, even while certain individuals may be infrequently mentioned by name in the text their views nonetheless form part of the empirical base for the generalizations as to group positions that follow.

While I have not used obviously political rhetoric, I have used arguments others might have been inclined to dismiss as mere rhetoric. Such arguments have been used when they made sense given the context of the time and their consistency with particular recovery theses and overall philosophical assumptions. Moreover, a simple fact must be continually kept in mind: the depression, the economic crisis, was *the* central problem and issue of these years. It provided the focus of a great public debate; it was a matter of the utmost urgency to the nation as a whole; it was the stimulus to a widespread discussion of alternatives wherein political leaders and others attempted to gain support for ideas and programs which they considered important or essential to the nation's recovery and prosperity. It is for this reason, too—the importance, centrality, pervasiveness, and urgency of the problem—

that the depression debate per se, the public airing of and controversy over divergent views, must be taken seriously.

Finally, in a study of this sort it is perhaps appropriate or even requisite for the author to indicate his own ideological frame of reference. I would not describe myself as New Left, traditional socialist, or orthodox liberal. This first persuasion, coming to the fore in the turmoil of the 1960s, was characterized by an admirable passion for social justice; unfortunately it was also characterized by an inadequate regard for political liberty and democratic processes, by a sometimes overly emotive or even irrational approach to the problems of the day, and by an extraordinary lack of historical perspective or understanding. Beyond the New Left, traditional American socialism, even of an indisputably democratic variety, has too often persisted in using rhetoric and concepts, and associating itself with ideological traditions, of dubious relevance to the American experience. In its most democratic versions, moreover, socialism's basic values are not unique to it but rather are those it derived from its own liberal heritage.

As to American liberalism, in its New Deal manifestation a major subject of this study, I adhere to its basic values—free inquiry, political liberty, democratic processes—but not to its barnacled economic dogmas. For American liberalism has never entirely freed itself from the capitalist dogmas with which its development was intertwined; it has never entirely freed its basic values from capitalist folklore; it has never entirely freed its propensity to experiment from the doctrinaire bounds provided by a simultaneous adherence to some concept of a capitalist "system." Liberalism would be truer to itself if it were simultaneously radical in the best sense—in the sense of going to the roots of problems free from dubiously relevant dogmas while adhering steadfastly to its own basic values. In the economic arena this would mean consideration of formulae allegedly noncapitalist but entirely democratic, a consideration of programs and policies allegedly radical but nonetheless rooted in American liberal ideals and traditions.

The study is organized topically. The initial chapter discusses major concepts and themes. Succeeding chapters outline the basic depression analyses and theories of recovery and relate these analyses and theories to more specific programmatic areas. A later chapter on economic "systems" places the debate in the larger ideological context. The final chapter provides an analysis and appraisal. For generalizations based upon extensive examples not presented here, and for lists of additional examples that are presented (mainly in notes), the reader is referred for documentation to my 1970 University of Wisconsin doctoral dissertation, "Roads to Recovery: The Economic Ideas of American Political Leaders, 1933–1938."

I wish to thank Paul Conkin, David P. Thelen, and R. Jackson Wilson for critical readings of the dissertation draft of this study. I owe a very special debt to Warren I. Susman for his generous help during a critical period, and for the inspiration he has long provided both as teacher and scholar. I owe my greatest debt to E. David Cronon for supervising this study as a dissertation, reading and criticizing subsequent versions, and providing invaluable support, counsel, and encouragement over the course of a decade.

DOGMA, DEPRESSION, AND THE NEW DEAL

PROLOGUE
From the 1930s to the 1970s

The depression of the 1930s came to an end, but it was never really solved. From the perspective of later, prosperous decades, the depression years were only too well remembered, the kind of memory that people wished to but never could wholly forget. It was a memory of the grim reality of 1933: estimates of thirteen million workers unemployed (no one had a precise figure), a national income which had plummeted by tens of billions of dollars, the failures of thousands of banks, the loss of hundreds of thousands of farms. It was a memory of a depression worse than any since that of the 1890s, a depression which left a legacy of underlying anxiety, a deep concern with retaining the prosperity of the post-1940 years, and perhaps an unwillingness to inquire too closely into the means through which that prosperity was sustained.

There was considerable concern, of course, during World War II and the early postwar period, over the possibility of a renewed depression. Liberal groups, moving away from the structural emphases of the previous decade, placed increasing emphasis on Keynesian fiscal policies to meet any crisis. Some business groups, such as the Committee for Economic Development, likewise moved away from the more divisive thirties and advanced their variants of Keynesian formulae. But the postwar boom,

3

despite a recession in 1949, continued into the 1950s. And during that decade, after years of economic prosperity and growth, fears of a postwar depression receded. Keynesian fiscal techniques, plus such built-in stabilizers or "cushions" as social security payments and unemployment compensation, it was increasingly held, had "solved" the problem of depression. Economic growth obviated any need for a basic redistribution of income: with growth everyone would receive a larger absolute if not relative share.

The culmination of this Keynesian era came in the prosperous and stable years of 1961–65, soon to be upset, however, by the economic impact of the Vietnam War. By the late 1960s, and into the 1970s, as inflation and recession threatened the economy simultaneously, the Keynesian remedies intellectually in vogue since the late 1930s and the 1940s were being called into question as to their contemporary adequacy. This, in turn, raised questions as to the solutions for economic crisis espoused and utilized since 1940: was the problem of depression ever really solved? What role did the unique historical circumstances of the post-1940 era play? From the perspective of the early 1970s, therefore, the depression decade of the 1930s took on a somewhat different look, and the divide between that decade and the postwar period seemed less decisive than in the 1950s and early 1960s.

Three intertwined questions seemed particularly worthy of attention: the genuineness of postwar prosperity, the related question of the impact of military and other "abnormal" expenditures, and the further related conclusiveness of the Keynesian remedy. As to the first, following satisfaction of the backlog built up during the war, there was the question of how and why the postwar boom continued, the question of the impact on the economy of such special demands as those created by the Marshall Plan (and foreign aid generally) and by military expenditures for hot wars and cold. Concern was initially expressed over what would follow when the "abnormal" circumstances of the early postwar period abated. A report of the liberal Americans for Democratic Action, for example, cautioned in 1947 that "Business has been sustained and stimulated by a number of abnormal factors which cannot be expected to last much longer."[1] But in one form or another, and most particularly in military form, they did.

Questions were raised, although less often as the 1940s gave way to the 1950s, about the economic impact and implications of vast military expenditures. Liberal economist Seymour Harris suggested in 1949, for example, that the prosperity of the 1940s had not really provided a resolution, that it was easy to maintain prosperity "by embarking on a vast destructive orgy once in twenty-five years and, in between the wars, by preparing for another struggle."[2] Rexford G. Tugwell added in 1952 that "Military expenditures had kept the economy going for more than a decade," that the "economy had become dependent on . . . a military market," and that "The end or even a diminution of military spending . . . frightened everyone who contemplated it."[3] Tugwell's voice, however, in the context of the 1950s, was a rather lonely one. In the wake of the Korean conflict and the hardening of the cold war, and in the wake of the economic assumptions of the 1950s that the problem of depression had been solved, the economic impact of military spending was not the subject of intense critical focus.

The altered mood of more recent years, however, has facilitated renewed discussion. British economist Joan Robinson, for example, noted in 1970 how arms expenditures could be seen as a de facto "solution of the problem of maintaining economic stability," and that "Whatever its causes, the consequence of the Cold War was to provide an outlet for government expenditure which did not compete with private enterprise and which did not saturate demand by producing anything that the public could consume."[4] American economist John Kenneth Galbraith similarly commented in 1970 that "The Keynesian economy relies to a disconcerting degree on military expenditures."[5] And one need not believe that the cold war was started as a device to preserve capitalist prosperity, nor take a New Left or neo-Stalinist view of the origins of that conflict, to focus on the economic impact of military expenditures, to query whether the prosperity of the postwar epoch was not based in the final analysis upon such expenditures, and to speculate as to the effectiveness of Keynesian formulae—not in theory but in the real institutional world—in some context other than that provided by cold war spending.

Keynesianism, of course, apart from its military application, was also utilized in conservative versions—for example, in tax reductions for business to spur the economy rather than in public spending on social needs. And with the concomitant emphasis on economic growth it evaded the question of income redistribution, a major concern of the 1930s to be heard again in the 1970s. As economist Daniel Fusfeld put it in 1972, the prevalent belief of the 1950s and 1960s was that progress and prosperity could be had "without rocking the boat by redistributing income or breaking up the great industrial and financial centers of power. The structure of wealth and power would remain untouched."[6] This last point—the role of corporate power—was also central to the 1930s debate and heard again in the 1970s. For it seemed increasingly clear by the 1970s that Keynesian techniques did not meet the problem of corporate power, of corporations which could set or "administer" their own prices, of an economy rigidified as to certain prices and thus susceptible to maladies, such as inflation with recession, not simultaneously remediable by fiscal policy. Reconsiderations thus brought together some basic concerns linking the 1970s to the 1930s and raised a central question as to the extent to which the "remedies" of the decades between were indeed really remedies at all.

1

THE RECOVERY DEBATE
Ideology and Tradition

The recovery debate was carried on within the context of a truly deep depression—a depression which by 1933 had lasted for over three years, worsening with each passing year, a depression which raised grave questions as to whether it was merely a downturn or rather a new stage, a transitory phenomenon or one with fundamental implications for America's economic institutions and ideology. The country's initial reaction, of course, was that the depression would be but temporary, that prosperity would shortly return, that the economy was (in the words of President Herbert Hoover) "fundamentally sound." This early reaction turned in time to stubborn rigidity among those who continued to hold it, and to a rethinking for those who came in time to reject it. The depression reached its nadir in 1933; the economy seemed to respond to the New Deal's stimuli; the nation began its slow recovery climb of 1934, 1935, and 1936: by mid-decade some were talking of the "recovery" which had been "achieved," though others warned that the basic maladjustments remained. The recession of 1937 sparked the debate anew, but the European crisis and the foreign policy controversy fast took center stage in 1939 and thereafter.

The New Deal itself was a complex phenomenon. The administration's early emphasis—the "first" New Deal—revolved

7

around the National Recovery and Agricultural Adjustment administrations. These were efforts to provide a measure of order to
a seemingly chaotic economy, to correct the system's central maladjustments, to spur the return of good times. This central NRA-
AAA effort was complemented by fiscal and monetary policies; it
was predicated upon the assumption (in the case of NRA) that
large-scale enterprise was here to stay, and that business and
government should "work together"; it was a concerted—though
not very well coordinated—attempt to revive and order the economy through means which went beyond those of the Hoover
regime yet remained essentially within the bounds of American
tradition and orthodoxy. The NRA, of course, was declared unconstitutional in 1935; the Supreme Court's rejection of the AAA
followed in early 1936. The political climate, too, changed during
these years; a gap between the New Deal and the greater part of
the business community developed and deepened. The administration turned away from business-government "cooperation" and
toward a revival of antimonopolism—the so-called "second" New
Deal. The stated objective became restoration of a competitive
economy; monopoly, the argument went, was the real barrier to
recovery. Public spending, too, became ever more central and
with the recession of 1937–38 it moved to the fore of the New
Deal's program.

There was, however, a central unity to the New Deal which
has too often been beclouded by the stress on economic structure.
Granted that there was a considerable distinction between planning and antimonopoly, the crucial point is that there was a basic
consistency to the New Deal rationale through these years. The
New Dealers as a group—or at least the New Deal political leaders—agreed as to their fundamental depression analysis: the key
problem, they argued, lay in the maldistribution of income; the
key need was, somehow, to provide a more equitable distribution
of income. This analysis, the purchasing power thesis, was as
central to New Deal planning in 1933–34 as it was to New Deal
antimonopolism in 1937–38. Seen in this light the differences between the first and second New Deals become in good part disagreements over method, disagreements over how best to implement a commonly held analysis.

Similarly, recent historical analyses have placed too much stress upon conservative divergences. Alf Landon, far from being the "Kansas Coolidge" of old, has practically been turned into a Kansas New Dealer. Herbert Hoover has been metamorphosed into some variety of "progressive." Yet despite some 1930s conservatives' antecedents as pre-World War I progressives (to be sharply distinguished from those characterized as progressives during the depression), and despite differences before 1933 and after 1938, there was on the question of recovery per se a basic unity to the conservative opposition to the New Deal. There were, to be sure, disagreements—Lewis Douglas, for example, contended that President Hoover had not adhered rigorously enough to classical economy formulae—but the cohesion over the idea that a lack of business confidence lay behind the depression's persistence was more central and more significant. The Douglases, the Hoovers, the Landons—regardless of their antecedents—all spoke the basic conservative language of the thirties.

The gap between these conservatives and the New Deal has been obscured by two factors, one chronological, the other substantive. First, there has been a tendency to read the New Era of earlier years and the Modern Republicanism of later years into the thirties; second, there is the nature of the New Deal itself. While there was a considerable cleavage between conservatives and New Dealers in their basic analyses of the depression, between the confidence and purchasing power theses, some differences between conservatives and New Dealers were more differences of degree than of kind. The key was the relationship between the New Dealers' basic analysis and the methods they used—and refused to use—to implement that analysis. No more than the conservatives would they consider public ownership of key industries or central planning by government, for example, though their basic analysis—unlike that of the conservatives—logically cohered with at least a consideration of these methods. In this sense traditional ideology played as large a role in shaping—and limiting—the New Dealers' specific responses to the depression as it did those of the conservatives.

Moreover, while much of the division over basic analyses was between adherents of the confidence and purchasing power theses, two other basic remedies were offered. These were the money cure and the exports cure. These remedies had their hardcore proponents, but they also proved attractive to others. This last point is crucial. For while the purchasing power thesis was central to the New Deal-progressive analysis, and, as Raymond Wolters has argued, "microscopic examinations of conflicting New Deal viewpoints tend to obscure the amount of consistency and direction that was present,"[1] the fact remained that New Dealers and progressives simultaneously refused to consider "radical" programs to implement that thesis and were at times attracted by the "easier" remedies of exports stimulation or currency manipulation. The New Deal administration did support Cordell Hull's trade program; the president did use monetary formulae to attempt to raise prices.

Outside of the political sphere, of course, there was a great deal of lively intellectual ferment in the thirties. Especially in the early New Deal years there was much enthusiastic talk of economic planning; there were visions of a new social and economic order; there was sharp questioning of the traditional American ethos. But all this had relatively little impact on the country's political leaders; among them the pull of tradition was strong; what influenced them most were the ideas which they inherited. Various political leaders, some of whom had received their political-ideological baptism in the 1890s, thus insisted again and again that the key to the depression lay in monetary policy, in the "money problem"; this was a persistent strain in the American tradition and it appeared repeatedly in the thirties. Another persistent strain was exports expansion; this, too, had a hardy tradition and was once again stubbornly set forth. Another strain was the horror over deficit spending and a ballooning federal debt. But the central tradition—and the most crucial influence of tradition—lay in certain overall American assumptions about the economy: that private enterprise was somehow more virtuous than public enterprise, that central planning and dictatorship somehow followed in logical and inevitable sequence, that free enterprise and political liberty were somehow intertwined and inseparable.

The New Dealers steadfastly clung to this central tradition—

to these traditional beliefs—at least in degree; they differed with conservatives as to where to draw the line beyond which the country could not safely go, but they, too, drew such lines; they denounced and rejected schemes on much the same traditional and dogmatic grounds that conservatives rejected their own programs. The New Dealers' basic analysis, the purchasing power thesis, and their basic values, which Franklin Roosevelt summarized as "democracy, humanity, and civil liberties," easily cohered. Their analysis was implicitly "radical"; their values by no means excluded "radical" programs. But dogmatic restrictions on the New Dealers' thinking prevented them from following through in the sphere of practical action. For although the New Dealers were democrats they did not effectively challenge an institutional structure which left basic economic decisions affecting the entire community in the hands of men not democratically responsible to that community. Although they were humanitarians they did not basically confront or resolve their fundamental problem: the inability of a rich nation to distribute the fruits of its abundance. And although they espoused the implicit egalitarianism of the purchasing power thesis, their simultaneous adherence to the capitalist "system" meant that certain redistributive measures could be neither considered nor adopted.

The "folklore of capitalism" was thus the dominant economic tradition in America. But there was also America's political tradition—democracy, egalitarianism, political liberty. To those who thought in terms of inclusive "social systems" America was an anomaly. Was it essentially a capitalist nation in which democracy was more or less a facade? Or was it both capitalist and democratic, a joining together of two essentially incongruous traditions, which many yet considered compatible and intertwined? In fact it was both capitalist and democratic, a land both of capitalist "freedom" and political liberty. The New Dealers, in a world beset by autocracy, renewed the country's faith in its political tradition, in its heritage of political liberty and democracy. There was nothing in *that* tradition and *that* heritage which conflicted with their economic analyses; indeed it was that tradition and heritage which embodied their basic values. There was no tampering with political liberty under the guise of "emergency."

But to the New Dealers the nation's economic and political traditions were inextricably linked. They were considered parts of a single tradition: capitalism *was* democratic; democracy *was* capitalist; America was a "capitalist democracy." The New Dealers did not follow through on the implications of America's democratic political tradition in the economic arena. Radicals, too, sometimes placed America's economic and political traditions into a single category; they sometimes argued that civil liberties were "hollow," that they were "not worth having," in a capitalist socioeconomic order. Capitalism was to them *the* overriding reality; political institutions were only tools of the "ruling class"; political democracy under such conditions was a mere sham. But the need was not uncritically to accept capitalism in the name of democracy (as the New Dealers did), nor to brush aside political liberty in the name of socialism (as some radicals did), but to examine critically the alleged link between the two traditions.

This failure to examine critically the alleged link between capitalism and democratic liberty went to the heart of much of the dogmatism and imprudence of American radicalism, whether in its 1930s Marxist or 1960s New Left version. And it went to the heart of much of the ambivalence and ambiguity of modern American liberalism and of American liberal historiography. For the ambivalence and ambiguity of modern liberals, liberal historians, and the New Dealers as heirs and transmitters of the liberal tradition was due in large part to the extent to which liberals have shared conservative assumptions and conservative modes of thinking, and to the extent to which the sharing of these assumptions and these modes of thinking has stymied and limited the implementation of basic liberal values and analyses.

New Dealers, their predecessors, and their successors, often focused upon the undemocratic political implications of private economic power. The New Dealers, in the context of the recovery problem, were well aware of the adverse impact of the exercise of private economic power upon their efforts. A leading liberal historian of the New Deal, Arthur Schlesinger, Jr., has viewed much of American history as a struggle between business and other groups in the community. But due to dogmatic blinders of their own, liberals have tended not to follow through on the implications of their analyses. While conservatives have argued that liberal intervention in the economy was paving the way for dictatorship, liberals in turn have declared that more "radical" intervention in the economy would prove to be the road to totalitarianism. In other words, modern liberals have tended to share the conservatives' dogmatic assumption that "too much" government economic intervention of itself led to totalitarianism, differing only as to where to draw the abysmal line.

There were two basic roots of the liberals' adherence to this essentially conservative and dogmatic belief. First, capitalism and democracy, business and political liberty, developed contemporaneously in America; and while capitalist liberty resulted in an economic monopolism antagonistic (in the view of many) to political democracy, the nexus in American thinking was never really unjoined. The thought was that economic freedom, defined in individualistic terms, went hand in hand with the individual's political right of free expression. A second and more immediate source of this adherence applied with special force to New Dealers in the late 1930s, and to liberals and liberal historians of the post-World War II era. This was the rise of European totalitarianism. In the wake of fascist and communist horrors, and in reaction against them, liberals recoiled from any form of economic collectivism, from any form of economic planning beyond that of the Keynesian variety (except for "emergencies"), and from any critical examination of the basically conservative assumption that "socialism" and democratic political freedoms were incompatible.

Arthur Schlesinger, Jr., for example, in his well-known *Age of Roosevelt,* applied to the New Deal in the late 1950s the basic liberal tenets he had been preaching since the 1940s. Schlesinger argued, as a leading spokesman for postwar American liberalism, that the European experience, both fascist and communist, had demonstrated the totalitarian potential in economic collectivism and central economic planning per se. He further contended that America's New Deal provided a "mixed economy" alternative which permitted enough government intervention (largely in the form of Keynesianism and the welfare state) to prevent depression and alleviate the problems of social injustice, while avoiding

the totalitarian perils allegedly inherent in "too much" intervention.[2]

Yet this interpretation of the New Deal, flowing from the
fearful and conservative mood of postwar liberalism, left key
questions both unasked and unanswered. Just what was the relationship between economic collectivism or planning per se and
the rise of totalitarianism in Europe? Was it causal? Did totalitarianism spring from economic or rather from cultural-political
factors and traditions? Did Germany, Russia, and Italy succumb
to totalitarianism in part because they, unlike America, lacked a
strong cultural-political tradition of democracy, political liberty,
and constitutionalism? What was the relationship between the
existence of such a cultural-political tradition, economic collectivism, and the danger of totalitarianism? New Dealers rejected conservative charges that Roosevelt's programs would lead
to totalitarianism. Yet New Dealers, and their modern liberal
heirs, made the very same attack upon those who called for more
radical economic programs than their own. The mode of thinking
was the same; the dogmatism was the same; only the drawing of
the line beyond which lay the abyss differed.

The concept of a "mixed economy" (essentially a postwar
term) or "middle way" (a 1930s term) which Schlesinger applied
to the New Deal also had its ambiguities and limitations. There
could, after all, be all kinds of mixed economies and all kinds of
middle ways. What was to be the mix? Which was to be *the*
middle way? These vague phrases were (and are) of distinctly
limited utility in analyzing either modern American liberalism in
general or the New Deal in particular. One could move to the left
of the basic program of postwar American liberalism and still remain an advocate of some variety of mixed economy. One could
move to the left of Franklin Roosevelt's New Deal and still remain
an advocate of some variety of middle way.

This leads to the realm of the allegedly nonideological nature of American liberalism and to the allegedly pragmatic character of the New Deal. Schlesinger has stressed the intellectual
rigidity of both the Marxist left and the conservative right and
the pragmatism and flexibility of the New Dealers. Rejecting the
either-or concept of mutually exclusive economic systems, he has

argued, the New Dealers proceeded through the use of experimental techniques and instrumentalities.[3] Some recent writers, in various ways, have challenged this concept of New Deal pragmatism. Howard Zinn, for example, has argued that while the New Dealers may have been flexible in their use of techniques, they were limited in their concept of goals.[4] Paul Conkin, following Rexford Tugwell, has stressed Franklin Roosevelt's individual intellectual limitations and blinders.[5]

Yet the basic point is that the New Dealers were themselves at times dogmatic, that they were dogmatic about techniques rather than goals, and that Franklin Roosevelt was by no means unique in this regard. The New Dealers' dogmatism was not that of a highly intellectualized system, to be sure, as was the case with Marxists; but dogmatism has practical implications, complications, and consequences, even when relatively unschematized, even when implicit rather than explicit, even when vague rather than precise. To reject alternative programs as allegedly leading in some vague and nebulous way to totalitarianism (as the New Dealers did) is quite as damaging to the practical implementation of such programs as a highly schematized, highly intellectualized rationale for rejection.

In fact the New Dealers were not (in their own terms) pragmatic and nonideological enough. The New Deal had "radical" implications, and it conceivably could have followed through on these implications in a pragmatic and nonideological way, in a way which would have constituted a fuller use and version of the very techniques which liberal historians later attributed to it. To suggest that the New Deal was pragmatic as to means but limited as to ends ignores the fact that people of all persuasions set ambitious goals—an economy of abundance, an economy of plenty, and so on—but that the New Dealers (as well as conservatives) dogmatically rejected potential programs geared to reach these goals. In the end, moreover, the New Dealers too easily succumbed to the vision of a goal which blurred their view of the means used to attain it. Prosperity came to America after 1940 not through a redistribution of income but through war; and it remained after 1945 not through a redistribution of income but through an era of cold war.

One side of the pragmatic coin thus deals with the process of rejection, and New Dealers, like the conservatives, dogmatically rejected alternative programs when such programs were deemed ideologically beyond the pale, when they were deemed incompatible with the "capitalist system," when they allegedly would threaten "regimentation," "bureaucracy," and autocracy— all horrors which conservatives in their turn insisted would ensue from the New Deal's own programs. The other side of the pragmatic coin deals with the process of systemic examination. There is a difference between uncritically (and either implicitly or explicitly) thinking in terms of economic "systems" and rejecting potential programs as contrary to the given "capitalist system," on the one hand, and critically examining a given set of institutional arrangements and interconnections (or "system") on the other. The New Dealers did the first and thus were unpragmatic in their process of rejection; they failed to do the second and thus were unpragmatic in their process of systemic examination. Theirs was an "exclusive" rather than an "inclusive" pragmatism.

The prime example of this exclusive pragmatism lay in the New Dealers' attempts to implement the purchasing power thesis even as their efforts were continually stymied by an institutional reality (the extent of private economic power) whose logical implications they failed fully to grasp given their firm commitment to the continuance of the "capitalist system." The New Dealers wanted to implement the purchasing power thesis, they wanted to preserve their version of the "capitalist system," and they never resolved the question of how to do both. Public ownership and central planning were dogmatically rejected as contrary to that "system," but the purchasing power thesis called for a more equitable distribution of income. How could the thesis be implemented while remaining within the bounds of the "capitalist system"? How could it be implemented given the basic powers held by private corporations? The New Dealers, all through their years of power, tried to implement the thesis without violating the bounds of their concept of capitalism. They remained, in their own lights, frustrated in this effort. What they tried to do corporate power would undo. To challenge corporate power, not only in terms of antimonopoly but also in terms of public planning and ownership, was beyond their ideological bounds. The admitted evils of corporate power, as seen by New Dealers, could thus not be met at least in part because of the ideological strictures of the New Dealers themselves.

For the New Dealers were doubly perplexed. They failed to examine capitalism as a "system," the concept of system here used for the complex of institutional arrangements and interconnections. And they wanted to preserve what they either implicitly conceived of or explicitly referred to as the "capitalist system," refusing whether implicitly or explicitly even to consider programs which they deemed to be either inherently outside or contrary to that "system." They thought in terms of discrete instrumentalities when (given their own values and analyses) they should have thought in terms of a "system"—in the process of examining the economy. And they thought in terms of "systems" when (given their own values and analyses) they should have thought in terms of discrete instrumentalities—in the process of considering practical programs. The New Dealers, in other words, assumed the "capitalist system" as given instead of examining it in terms of an inclusive pragmatism, and they rejected such programs as public ownership and central planning as contrary to the existing "system" rather than considering them pragmatically as potential techniques to implement their depression analyses.

Moreover, to say that the "system" of the 1930s (or of the present) was and is essentially "capitalist"—basic powers remain in private hands—does not mean that the alternative can or should be described as "socialist" (with all that term implies); that is, one can call the existing system "capitalist" in terms of its basic characteristics and not see "socialism" or any other "ism" as *the* alternative. One can instead think of altering that system through certain programs (such as public ownership and central planning) apart from any concept of "socialism"; indeed such programs could be conceived of as an extension of America's democratic political tradition. And a mixed economy, again, can come in many mixes. Minnesota's Farmer-Labor Governor Floyd Olson, for example, critical of capitalism, suggested in 1932 that "We have now reached the socialized state. Just how far it shall extend its functions and services is no longer a matter of theory but

a problem of practice and expediency."[6] Olson was to criticize
the New Deal from the left, yet also eschew orthodox socialism.
Here was an alternative middle way which might have been
considered on pragmatic grounds.

Several other key related themes ran through the debate,
further illuminating the dogmatism-pragmatism question. The
concept of "artificial prosperity," the idea of an abnormally based
boom, was advanced in several versions. It was used to dismiss
devices more radical than those desired (or to rationalize those
accepted only for the "emergency"), and in this way could be a
dogmatic concept. It was also used to characterize earlier "easy"
routes to prosperity, and in this way could be an analytical concept. Here, too, as in the case of the purchasing power thesis per
se, there was a gap between analyses and programs: political
leaders were forever tempted by "easy" ways out, some of which,
in terms of their own analyses, had earlier led to a disastrous and
ephemeral artificial prosperity. And the question remained as to
whether the depression gave way in the end to another era of
artificial prosperity, a prosperity which, however, after World
War II, came itself to be defined as the "norm."

"Balance" was another leading concept of the thirties. The
New Dealers, historical analyses have run, sought a "balanced
economy," and the phrase has been used as if it were a key to the
New Deal approach and the epitome of the New Deal rationale.
But the idea of a balanced economy was less a key than a clue.
For while it was a central New Deal concept, it was also used in
varying ways by progressives, radicals, and conservatives. Everyone, after all, could call for a balanced economy; the key question
was, how was the economy to be balanced? There were as many
answers to this question as there were programs for recovery. The
balanced economy concept, therefore, like the related concept of
economic interdependence, took on meaning only in relation to
more specific formulae. Of itself, "balanced economy," like
"middle way," was less an analytical concept than a nonanalytical
evasion.

The "emergency rationale" provided another clue to the
character of the recovery debate and thus of the American ideological tradition. The tendency to agree to unorthodox programs

only on an "emergency" basis showed an unwillingness to consider whether the emergency itself might be of a more permanent nature, and showed also the ideological inhibitions involved in refusing to accept unorthodox formulae as permanent reforms rather than as merely temporary devices. Moreover, it raised several further questions. How could calls for the repeal of emergency "expedients" be answered when the immediate crisis was over yet the basic problem remained? How were such expedients to be defended, when their foes had a text and a writ with which to demand repeal once the emergency had passed? How, following repeal of the expedients, could consequent "emergencies" then be analyzed and resolved?

Finally, there was the pervasive "antiplanning" concept. There was, of course, strong and vocal opposition to the planning philosophy among conservatives. But by "antiplanning" is meant something more subtle than this. Antiplanning refers to the way in which proponents of various remedies and programs offered them as "easy" ways out, as solutions consistent with America's ideological norms, as measures specifically geared to avoid the rigors of planning—and thereby in turn the horrors of "bureaucracy" and "regimentation." Antiplanning thus further evidenced the tenacity of traditional ideology, the tendency to evade hard questions, the quest for easy remedies, the gap between analysis and implementation—withal the basic defining characteristics of the political leaders' recovery debate.

2

ROOTS OF THE DEBATE

The roots of the debate over recovery centered on the concept of economic maturity, a concept derived from an analysis of America's economic past, a concept with far-reaching implications for America's economic future. Espoused by various New Dealers, progressives, and radicals, it led squarely to the purchasing power thesis. Implicitly it led beyond: radicals saw it as a basis for a new economic "system." Its epochal implications were sharply rejected by conservatives. The key departure from the "norm" in their view (based upon classical economy and confidence thesis assumptions) was the New Deal itself. Further concepts developed in this context included the idea of "artificial prosperity" and the idea that Americans historically had tried to find "easy" ways out of their hard dilemmas. The question posed was, would Americans now truly confront or again try to escape from their problems? In terms of the logic of those who espoused the mature economy theme (if not in terms of their practical applications), the time had now come at last for just such a confrontation.

As the depression persisted through the years, as times became worse—culminating in the crisis of 1933—rather than better, the optimism of the first months following the crash gave way among some to a view that the depression was no mere crash or panic, that it marked an epochal stage in the history of capitalism, that it reflected deep-seated and organic changes in the economic order. This view was expressed both in economic theory and in the economic thinking of political leaders. Opposed to this view, which reflected the pessimism of the time, was a second, which reflected the pertinacity of the time. As economists and politicians of the left advanced the economic maturity thesis, economists and politicians of the right reaffirmed the verities of classical theory, steadfastly arguing that the downturn was but temporary and that its severity was due to factors external to the system itself.

A basic cleavage, then, lay between those who saw the depression as the end of one era and the beginning of another in the nation's history, and those who denied the reality of such a sharp break with the past; between those who advanced the mature economy theme (given its most famous political expression in Franklin Roosevelt's 1932 Commonwealth Club address), and those who rejected it; between various radicals, progressives, and New Dealers, on the one hand, and conservatives on the other. In the past, the economic maturity argument went, an open frontier and a rapidly growing population had provided the basis for an expanding economy. Now the frontier had disappeared and the population was becoming stationary. Technological advance had brought unemployment. In the past external expansion of the economy was possible; now this possibility was rendered nugatory by the sweep of economic nationalism across the world.

The mature economy theme, this epochal view of the economic order, was expressed in at least some measure by such modern progressives as Senators Robert M. La Follette, Jr., and Bronson Cutting, and by such New Deal Democrats as Michigan Governor Frank Murphy and New York Congressman James Mead.[1] Pennsylvania's New Deal Governor George Earle argued that during the nineteenth century economic expansion was so great "that labor-saving devices were not a problem. Then . . . our expansion began rapidly to slacken"; technological unemployment appeared. ". . . we had . . . exploited our resources. Our frontier

days were over. There was no more room for expansion."[2] New
York Mayor Fiorello La Guardia sketched a striking picture of
the implications of a mature economy: "We have no frontiers
now. The country is built. There are no promising markets in the
world awaiting our goods. What are we going to do?"[3]

Such New Dealers as Alabama Senator Hugo Black and relief
administrator Harry Hopkins also expressed representative versions of this theme. In the past, as Black saw it, "the rapid . . .
growth of our population, the influx of immigrants, and the
availability of new lands constantly opened new opportunities for
employment and new and enlarged markets for the products of
our farms and factories. But in more recent years the natural
growth of our population has slackened, the flow of immigration
has abated, the frontier of new lands has disappeared." These
changed conditions, aggravated by the contagion of economic
nationalism and the economic impact of technology, "have made
it much more difficult . . . for workers to find a market for their
labor and . . . for industry and agriculture to find a market for
their products." The economy could now "be stabilized and
strengthened only if we find . . . means of utilizing . . . productivity . . . to raise the standard of living of our existing population."[4]

Harry Hopkins argued that "as a Nation we refused for
many years to recognize basic changes which were taking place
in our economic structure. . . . We seem to have assumed there
was no end to anything. . . . Those who could find no economic
place for themselves moved West until there were no more
frontiers. Our foreign trade dropped off as . . . other nations
strove for economic self-sufficiency. We built up our industrial
plant until its machines could produce more than our income
pattern would let us consume."[5] To men such as Earle, La
Guardia, Black, and Hopkins, the logic of a new stage led to the
necessity of a New Deal—reforms and readjustments to revive
and reorder the economy. It signaled the end of capitalism's expansionist phase, but not of capitalism itself; it called for a new
emphasis on consumptive rather than on productive faculties,
an "intensive" expansion in consumptive capacity to replace the
"extensive" geographic expansion of the past.

To radicals, the new economic stage marked the collapse of capitalism and heralded the coming of a new socioeconomic order. This was the radical and socialist version—and use—of the mature economy theme. Milwaukee's Socialist Mayor Daniel Hoan, for example, argued that this depression was unlike its predecessors. In the past, he contended, "there was free land to absorb the unemployed," or new industries to absorb capital, or war. None of these were now present. ". . . Evidence that this is a permanent problem is obvious. . . ."[6] Socialist party leader Norman Thomas held that the capitalist crisis was rooted in the frontier's closing, the stabilization of population, economic nationalism, income maldistribution, and the failure of a new industry to appear as in past depressions to lead the way to recovery. All these made it impossible for capitalism to function as it did when it was an expanding force.[7]

Wisconsin's radical Congressman Thomas Amlie viewed capitalism as an organism which grew only as long as it had room for expansion. First the western frontier, and with its closing, other frontiers kept the system going: the construction of railroads and great industries in the late nineteenth century; imperialism, which permitted the investment of capital abroad; spending for war, which stimulated prosperity; the scientific frontier and the advent of the automobile; and foreign loans to finance American exports. But this depression, Amlie argued, was terminal. There were no longer any land frontiers into which to expand; the frontier of world trade was permanently closed to expansion because of trade restrictions; and even if some great new invention such as the automobile appeared, it would be of little avail given the maldistribution of wealth. To Amlie, the nation faced "the stern reality of a frontier that has permanently disappeared."[8]

The frontier thesis constituted an integral part of the mature economy theme; it also provided a basis for related views of the American economic past and present. The idea that in times past the frontier had provided a haven to which the economically distressed could go to repair their fortunes played an important role in the views taken toward unemployment by a number of New Dealers, progressives, and radicals. Governor Philip La

Follette, for example, held that "50 or 75 years ago, any periodic surplus of labor . . . could be absorbed in the new western lands. . . . The frontier was a safety valve. . . . Today that safety valve is gone."[9] House Speaker Henry Rainey lamented, "the land-vent is gone, and for a hundred years, and more, we had the most magnificent land-vent any country ever had. . . . There . . . [is] no more land to give away to the discontented."[10] This essential theme, with its obvious implications as a rationale for unemployment relief programs, was also sounded by such New Dealers and progressives as Roosevelt, Hopkins, Black, Bob La Follette, Secretary of Agriculture Henry Wallace, and Secretary of the Interior Harold Ickes.[11]

To some New Dealers, progressives, and radicals the frontier's key role per se explained both America's historic economic advance and the agonizing persistence of its present depression. In the past the nation's economic problems had in a measure been solved "by opening up new frontiers," Montana Congressman Roy Ayers put it, "but when we had no more . . . frontiers, then we woke up to . . . the unsoundness of this economic system."[12] The corollary of this adaptation of the frontier thesis was clear: it provided a rationale for government economic intervention. The physical frontier was gone and with it the easy evasion of past economic problems; such problems could no longer be resolved "naturally"; they would now have to be resolved institutionally. Wisconsin Progressive Congressman Gerald Boileau summed up the case: ". . . we can no longer leave it to the frontier—it is now the duty of the . . . government to act."[13] Wallace, Ickes, and Roosevelt all agreed that the logic of the frontier's closing led to government economic intervention or planning.[14]

While conservatives generally attributed the paucity of capital investment to a lack of business confidence, those on the left utilized the frontier thesis to fashion an alternative explanation. Bob La Follette, for example, based much of his analysis of American capitalism upon this adaptation of the thesis. In the nineteenth century, he argued, the expanding frontier had continually offered opportunities for profitable capital investment, including the inducement for the investment of those "huge blocks of capital" which drew the economy out of past depressions. But without the inducement of the frontier the old method of pulling the economy out of depression would not work. The incentive for private capital investment had been so reduced that it could no longer "take place in a large enough volume to prevent our economy from contracting." The only way the country could now recover was for "Government . . . to provide the capital for capital expenditure purposes. . . ."[15]

Phil La Follette argued that the crucial economic change of the era was that "horizontal expansion" around the globe had been completed and the need now was to turn to "vertical development." Private capital investment worked only as long as "frontiers still beckoned for development. . . . It is a failure when the great enterprises are in the realm of housing . . . and other phases of life here at home. Purely private capital will invest horizontally, but it will not invest perpendicularly." The frontier's closing marked the end of the "old capitalism" and produced a stagnation of capital. That stagnation would continue until government acted to provide a new mechanism for capital investment. "The issue is not capitalism versus socialism or communism, but the solution of the problem produced by the disappearance of the frontier."[16]

A number of New Dealers argued that there was already an overexpansion of plants and factories (at least relative to effective consumer demand); therefore to put further capital into more factories would be to aggravate the problem. This argument was expressed by such men as Hugo Black, James Mead, Congressman Maury Maverick, and Senators Claude Pepper and Lewis Schwellenbach.[17] Franklin Roosevelt's best-known statement in this vein came in the Commonwealth Club address, but it was not an isolated expression. During the early years of the New Deal the President repeatedly asserted that in some lines—largely in the area of heavy industry—the country was overbuilt, the productive plant was greater than could be balanced by existing demand. Roosevelt therefore rejected "the orthodox . . . view that there is this flood of money waiting for investment" upon the restoration of confidence. "The Lord only knows where that money would go, I don't."[18]

Conservatives mounted an ideological attack upon the New

Deal-progressive-radical version of the frontier thesis and the economic maturity theme. It was, they charged, inherently defeatist, inherently pessimistic. This element of alleged defeatism in the New Deal—the idea that America's historic expansion had ended, that unemployment had become chronic—was rejected by such men as Herbert Hoover, 1936 GOP vice-presidential candidate Frank Knox, veteran Illinois Republican Frank Lowden, and Senators Frederick Steiwer and L. J. Dickinson.[19] Former Treasury Secretary Ogden Mills declared, "We must scotch the pernicious notion that the frontier is closed. Ours is still the land of opportunity. . . ."[20] Senator Walter George affirmed, "we are a young nation. . . . We are [not] always going to have unemployment. . . . In the future we will expand our industries to such an extent as will make radio and automobile and other . . . industries of the present of minor consequence. . . ."[21]

Alf Landon, Kansas Governor and 1936 Republican presidential candidate, particularly stressed this theme. The mature economy argument—that the economic crisis marked the end of the expansionist era, that government must play an increasingly important economic role—was not new, Landon insisted. It had been heard during the depression of the 1890s; it had not been true then; it was not true now. The end of the western frontier did not—in the nineties or the thirties—mark the end of the era of expansion; for in its place was the "new frontier" of new wants and inventions spiralling the economy to ever-greater levels of progress.[22] American capitalism retained its dynamism and could be renewed again; the problem was not loss of energy in the nation's economic system but loss of faith among its New Deal leaders.

Lewis Douglas, one-time Roosevelt administration budget director, thereafter a leading Democratic critic of the New Deal, argued that since the frontier did not disappear suddenly and since the population's rate of growth did not slacken all at once, the impact of these factors could easily be overestimated, "particularly since other countries . . . maintained a fair degree of prosperity in the face of no frontier at all and a diminishing population." Douglas further challenged the idea that the country's industrial plant was overbuilt. This, he argued, was not a new idea; it had been expressed during depressions for over a century; it had been proven wrong in every case. Every past depression had been conquered by capital consumption. Even if no new industry now emerged, the continual need for replacement would still provide great activity in the area of capital goods.[23]

To the assertion by adherents of the mature economy thesis that the disappearance of the physical frontier required the implementation of economic planning, conservative critics of the New Deal responded by pointing to the existence of other frontiers that could provide bases for further economic expansion. The roots of growth, they suggested, lay not in geography but in technology. This idea—that the new frontier of science was key—was particularly developed by Senator Henry Hatfield and by former President Hoover. Hatfield argued that chemical research and the industries based upon it offered "an unlimited field for new . . . activity." The creators of synthetic products through chemical research were today's pioneers, and there was "no geographical limit . . . for scientific pioneering." In contrast to the New Deal's adaptation of the frontier thesis, Hatfield stressed that the new employment created by chemical research "is . . . none of it . . . artificially stimulated."[24] Science was thus the true frontier, government economic intervention an "artificial" one.

Herbert Hoover continually criticized the economic maturity theme as evidencing a lack of faith not only in the economic system's vigor but in that of America itself. In his 1932 response to Roosevelt's Commonwealth Club address, for example, he challenged "the whole idea that . . . this country has reached . . . the height of its development." What Roosevelt had "overlooked is the fact that we are yet but on the frontiers of development of science . . . and . . . invention. . . ." "Progress . . . was not due to the opening up of new agricultural land; it was due to . . . scientific research, the opening of new invention. . . . There are a thousand inventions . . . in the lockers of science . . . which have not yet come to light; all are but on their frontiers."[25] Hoover repeated this argument again and again during the New Deal years, berating the economic maturity idea and the plans and paraphernalia based upon it.[26]

Conservatives—mostly of the Republican variety—presented an alternative explanation to the rejected mature economy theme. Their argument had four main parts: that the depression was worldwide, that it had in large measure been a consequence of the World War, that it was not otherwise unique among depressions, and that it had persisted because of New Deal policies. The theme that the American depression was part of an international crisis of international origins was expressed by such conservative Republicans as Herbert Hoover, Congressmen James Beck and Bertrand Snell, and Senators David Reed and Warren Austin.[27] Implicit in this view was the idea that the American economic system as such could not be held responsible for the depression, an idea embraced by such critics of the New Deal as Hoover, Republican Allen Treadway, and Democrat Joseph Ely.[28]

Those who viewed the depression as worldwide in its origins often pointed to the World War as its basic underlying cause.[29] The war provided an external and wholly reprehensible source for the depression, requiring change neither in the country's economic institutions nor in its ideology. Ogden Mills, for example, attributing the depression to the war, explicitly absolved the American economic system of culpability, adding that "once started . . . the pattern has not differed essentially from that of previous" crises.[30] The corollary of the contention that this depression was otherwise basically like those that had gone before was equally clear. What, asked Frank Lowden, justified the New Deal's "revolutionary" changes in government? "We have had serious depressions before."[31] Conservatives such as Henry Hatfield, Congressman Hamilton Fish, and Senator Josiah Bailey all similarly characterized the present crisis as only the latest in a long series of depressions.[32]

The denial that this depression was epochal led easily to the assertion that the "natural" return of prosperity had been arrested by the New Deal. The country had conquered depressions before, the refrain ran; why did this depression—among all others—persist? Herbert Hoover[33] was only one of the many

conservative Republicans who argued that the United States
along with other nations was coming out of the depression in
1932. Other countries continued to advance, the argument went,
but America's progress was held back by the 1932 election and
the advent of the New Deal. Among those expressing this theme,
at least in part, were Mills, Beck, and Frank Knox.[34] "The
American system is not at fault," Knox asserted in 1936. "Recovery was on its way four years ago."[35] The nations making the
greatest strides toward recovery, Senator Simeon Fess added,
were "those least affected by artificial remedies."[36] "Recovery
has come fastest," David Reed concluded, "in those lands . . .
which have seen the futility of trying to legislate prosperity. . . ."[37]

GOP House leaders Bertrand Snell and John Taber further
argued that there had been a revival of prosperity in the United
States in 1933—until the National Industrial Recovery and Agricultural Adjustment acts went into effect.[38] Others insisted that
such recovery as existed by 1936 dated from the Supreme Court's
decision invalidating the NRA, among them Hoover, Landon,
and Knox.[39] Michigan Senator Arthur Vandenberg declared in
1936 that any economic advance had been due to the natural
upswing of the business cycle; it had come in spite of rather than
because of the New Deal.[40] The New Deal's "planned economy"
in each case was seen as the very preventive of recovery; in each
case it was argued that the economy spurted toward recovery
freed from the restraints of such intervention—or in spite of
them. Landon, Knox, and Steiwer all echoed the charge that the
New Deal had retarded recovery; Hoover, Beck, and Bailey all
agreed that recovery would have come "naturally" had it not
been for governmental interference.[41]

Conservatives, then, provided an alternative to the idea that
the depression marked a sharp break with the past and that
government accordingly would be required to enlarge its economic role. Rejecting the radical implications of the frontier
thesis, they stood solidly upon the traditions of classical economics and limited government. Contending that the processes of
capitalism—unthwarted by those of government—would have
spiralled the economy toward recovery, they stressed the reality
of continuity in the past and the need for continuity in the pres-

ent. By the later thirties some New Dealers had also fastened upon a version of a continuous past, but they used it for a very different purpose: as yet another rationale for government economic intervention. American capitalism, they now argued, had long been supported by governmental props.

Robert Jackson and Harry Hopkins both expressed this theme. Jackson, a leading New Deal spokesman in 1937–38, argued that "American private enterprise has never been continuously self-sustaining. It has always operated under concealed subsidies. Until the end of the last century we operated a Works Progress Administration by which the unemployed could get a quarter section of public land just for occupying it." World War spending constituted the "second Works Progress Administration." "After the war came the third Works Progress Administration. We went into a foreign boondoggling program." The country no longer had "these costly but concealed subsidies to take up the slack in employment."[42] Hopkins, too, argued that American capitalism had historically been subsidized. Whether through public lands or foreign loans, he asserted, "Private enterprise has never been able to operate without governmental intervention. . . ."[43]

Tom Amlie, in 1938, by now a supporter of the Roosevelt administration, similarly argued that "American capitalism has never functioned without government subsidy. It took the form of free land, title to mineral rights, loans, and cash grants as long as the public domain lasted." Government subsidies to spur the economy could never again come "painlessly out of the frontier." They would now have to come out of taxation. "The easy way to meet the problem is gone, and only the hard way is left."[44] The "natural" remedy had vanished; the "institutional" remedy now required reallocation of the nation's resources. The "subsidization" version of America's economic past thus provided a precedent for intervention by government in America's economic present; the nineteenth-century "New Deal" had been inherent in the government's use of the public domain; the twentieth-century "New Deal" would use government once again to spur on the nation's economy.

There was an interesting connection between this concept

of a government-subsidized economic past and the various versions advanced in the thirties of the concept of "artificial prosperity." Hopkins, for example, held that the depression "did not come a number of years earlier . . . because, although the stage in this country was all set for it, we managed to keep up our prosperity through a succession of ingenious but destructive devices."[45] A number of New Deal-progressive leaders shared this view that the great depression had been postponed through the stimuli of war or foreign loans.[46] A further intriguing connection appeared between the usually Democratic assertions that the prosperity of the 1920s had been "artificial" because it was based upon foreign loans to create markets for American exports, and the anguished conservative cries that New Deal prosperity was "artificial" because it was based upon deficit spending by government.

Finally, there were those who argued that each recent era of prosperity had been sustained by some kind of external intervention. James Mead, for example, held that first through wartime spending, then through foreign loans, and finally through the New Deal, prosperity had been achieved.[47] New Deal Congressman Byron Harlan agreed that "The 1913 panic vanished in tremendous World War purchases; the one in 1920 disappeared in a $13,000,000,000 foreign loan to finance more foreign purchases. The panic in 1929 . . . disappeared in a $14,000,000,000 spending program."[48] Congressman John Dingell rather more partisanly contended that New Deal pump priming was not new, that the Republican administrations of the 1920s had "primed the pumps of foreign governments and foreign industries through the medium of fake bonds. . . ."[49] And Harold Ickes charged that during the twenties "Republican relief was lavished in foreign lands . . . in the form of . . . foreign loans." The New Deal's "Public Works Administration . . . invites a comparison. . . ."[50]

The concern over the lost geographic frontier, on the one hand, and over the decline of the export trade and the movement toward nationalism, on the other, were closely linked. Each posited, in effect, that the spurs or props or supports that

had activated and enlarged and enriched American capitalism
in the past—an expanding western frontier provided by the new
lands of a young nation, and the expanding export trade provided by the debtor status of a young nation—had ceased to
exist. The implications of this for the future of capitalism in
America were obvious and enormous. The geographic frontier
clearly could not be rediscovered; new exports frontiers seemed
highly unlikely in the thirties; the logical concomitant of both
factors seemed to many to be that the new frontier was at home.

To New Dealers and modern progressives, government intervention would now play the same role that the open frontier
had played in the past; it would cushion the impact of depression, provide succor for the unemployed, and work to renew
the economy. It would provide an institutional replacement for
a vanished geographical phenomenon. But while New Dealers
and progressives saw in the mature economy thesis a rationale
for economic policies designed to readjust and revamp the existing system, radicals saw in the mature economy thesis proof that
even such readjustments and revamping were doomed to fail,
that they—much less the conservatives' policies based upon the
very rejection of the mature economy assumptions—could not
save the system which had lost its dynamic, which had reached
its terminus.

Each group, on a wide range of issues, including the key
question as to whether a lack of "confidence" or purchasing
power lay behind the depression's persistence, utilized its view
of the depression in historical perspective as a basis for its explanation of and rationale for present assumptions, attitudes,
policies, and programs. To those who accepted the mature
economy thesis, such phenomena as a redistribution of income,
unemployment relief, and measures geared to social welfare
would all seem in order. For some, the mature economy theme
had implications for fiscal policy; government would have to act
because of the stagnation of private capital. It also had implications for farm and labor policy; if distressed farmers and
workers could no longer move west, new arrangements were now
imperative.

To those who denied the validity of the mature economy

thesis, who denied the western frontier a key role in America's economic past, who stressed the continuing role of expanding scientific rather than contracting geographic frontiers, who stressed that the crisis of the thirties was just another depression and not the end of a centuries-old era of capitalist expansion, and who moreover attributed the depression's severity to factors external to the "American system," all these mature economy assumptions could be and were rejected. To conservatives these ideas were merely knee-jerk reactions that occurred during times of depression—whether in the nineties or in the thirties—and could best be understood as gauges of pessimism rather than as measures of economic reality. They had been expressed before and had been proven wrong; the western frontier had disappeared years before in any case; other countries had prospered without geographical frontiers or growing populations.

Finally, some reformist leaders fashioned a continuous view of the past to fit the New Deal present. Such administration spokesmen as Robert Jackson and Harry Hopkins argued that New Deal economic intervention constituted a modernization of the American tradition: the government had always subsidized the economic system. To some the New Deal constituted a most beneficent modernization: if the New Deal had renewed prosperity, much as the spending for war and foreign loans of the twenties had, the New Deal's programs for "building up . . . America" (to use James Mead's phrase)[51] were far superior to the havoc of the war or the folly of the loans. Whether they could secure a genuine and lasting rather than an artificial and ephemeral prosperity remained a central, continuing question of the era.

3

DEPRESSION ANALYSES

The debate over the depression's origins had implications for the central controversy between proponents of the confidence and purchasing power theses. The confidence thesis applied the basic assumptions of the existing economic system to the conservative critique of the New Deal. The purchasing power thesis as an analysis drove to the roots of the assumptions of that system. The question remained, however, as to how the thesis could be implemented without threatening the continued existence of the system. Two alternative depression remedies—the exports cure and the money cure—evidenced the impact of traditional ideology and illustrated the persistence of efforts to find an "easy" solution to the crisis. The key purchasing power and confidence theses were further evident in the specific debate over the causes and cures of the recession of 1937–38. So, too, were they central to the debate over public spending. The New Deal's spending program derived from the purchasing power thesis: spending, the argument went, would distribute buying power pending implementation of the thesis through more permanent formulae. Based upon the purchasing power thesis, spending was sharply attacked by conservatives on the grounds of the confidence thesis. This debate gave further vent to the concept of artificial prosperity, to the emergency rationale, and to the idea of a "norm."

THE CONFIDENCE THESIS

The confidence thesis was the vital economic ingredient in American conservatism during the thirties and was echoed by conservatives (Democrats and Republicans alike) throughout the decade. It illustrated the persistence of classical economy assumptions in a period of tumult and depression (and it thereby further illustrated the traditionalism and dogmatism of those on the right); it was geared to a single class interest, that of business; rooted in classical theory, it further provided the rationale for very specific conservative programs and criticisms. It constituted, in other words, both a conservative theory to explain the failure of business to recover, and a conservative program to promote the recovery of business; it provided the conservative equivalent of the New Deal-progressive purchasing power thesis, as well as a conservative alternative to the New Deal-progressive-radical mature economy theme.

The confidence thesis, one of the most clearly intellectually rooted and systematic of all the ideological approaches taken by political leaders in the thirties, was thus the virtually exclusive lens through which conservatives viewed the events of the time and the inclusive interpretive schema into which conservatives placed them. A corollary of classical economics, it seemed at times virtually synonymous with laissez-faire: if the government ceased interference, if the New Deal stopped disruptive and destructive tinkering, the "natural forces" of recovery would soon revive prosperity. But it also took a step well beyond laissez-faire: government should not only cease its noisome tinkering, the refrain ran, but should act positively to nurture confidence. In either event, the confidence thesis provided the core of the conservative case against the New Deal, appearing in a wide variety of contexts, and running like an iron rod through the era.

Investment was the sine qua non of recovery, the thesis ran; and confidence triggered the propensity to invest. New Deal policies destroyed confidence, preventing investment and delaying recovery; among these policies were deficit spending, excessive taxation, currency tinkering, and harassment of business. Moreover, the very uncertainty surrounding New Deal experiments

and improvisations compounded the confusion. The requisite,
therefore, was to restore confidence by returing to fiscal orthodoxy, stabilizing the currency, and encouraging enterprise; this
would renew investment, ensuring recovery.

David Reed, Senator William H. King, and Frank Knox all
advanced the thesis. Reed declared in 1933 that "the quickest
relief that could be given . . . would be for Franklin D. Roosevelt
to come out today with the firm statement that . . . he will not
permit the . . . currency to be inflated. Should he do so there
would be such a boom as has not been seen for years."[1] King, a
Utah Democrat, prophesied that prosperity would return if government withdrew its heavy hand from the economy, reduced undue taxation, and stated to businessmen, " 'We intend to give
you a square deal. We intend that the Federal Government shall
not adopt socialistic policies. . . .' "[2] Knox summed up: "All
that . . . government can . . . or properly should do is to create
conditions under which confidence can be restored and private
. . . enterprise given a chance. . . ."[3]

The thesis was fully articulated by the bipartisan authors of
the 1937 "Conservative Manifesto."[4] It was also expressed by
Republicans Hoover, Vandenberg, Landon, Mills, and Snell.[5]
These Republicans were joined by a host of like-minded Democrats. Among them were Virginia's Senators Carter Glass and
Harry Byrd, Lewis Douglas, and Josiah Bailey.[6] All agreed, as
did the entire conglomeration of conservatives of the thirties, on
the validity of the confidence thesis both as a theory and as a
program; they expressed it with dogmatic certainty in virtually
their entire critique of the New Deal and its works.

The thesis had further implications for conservative positions
on democracy, the depression's origins, labor upheaval, and reform legislation. Representative Robert Rich, for example, at-
tacking the New Deal, asserted that "when the businessmen of
this country are ready to quit, when the 5 per cent of the people
who give employment to the other 95 per cent want to stop business, you are in a sad . . . plight in this country."[7] (This was a
conservative Republican's analysis. Others might have asked
whether the five per cent should have had such power over the
ninety-five per cent and over the nation's economy.) Ogden Mills

argued that the cessation of business buying of capital and durable goods was the immediate cause of the depression and the source of its persistence. "Why did business stop buying?" At decade's end, "suddenly doubt and hesitation appeared. The precise reason is difficult to ascertain."[8] (Critics were quick to exploit this confession. The New Deal, they pointed out, did not exist in 1929.)

Sit-down strikes were incorporated into the thesis as they came into vogue in 1937. Bailey, Knox, and Taber all agreed that they destroyed confidence and thereby struck at recovery.[9] Conservatives also utilized the recession of 1937–38 to resist further reform. Congressman Charles Eaton, for example, discussing wage-and-hour legislation, declared, "We are now in a . . . depression, and this is no time to introduce a bill of this kind and . . . disturb business already hampered by too much governmental interference."[10] GOP House leader Bertrand Snell concurred, arguing that "any more legislation that places more restrictions on business . . . makes it still harder . . . to put men back at work."[11] And Congressman Bruce Barton contended that a business-baiting course would "cause more upheaval and uncertainty and throw more people out of work."[12]

Socialist Norman Thomas argued that "One of the worst indictments of capitalism is its own wailing complaint that it cannot be reformed without being paralyzed." But Thomas, from the left, also accepted much of the confidence thesis as propounded by the right. He considered "lack of confidence . . . a great factor" in the 1937–38 recession. President Roosevelt, he asserted, contributed "to that lack of confidence . . . because of the uncertainties with regard to his future program. . . . Unquestionably there is a point where taxes and regulations which reduce the hope of profit, and policies which . . . inspire among . . . investors 'lack of confidence,' do keep money out of business. . . . The difficulty is that there is no mathematical formula for finding in advance the precise point beyond which this governmental regulation of the profit system cannot safely go."[13]

New Deal-progressive critics of the thesis remarked that government-business relations were amicable through the twenties, and yet the crash came in 1929. They noted that Herbert

Hoover was friendly toward business, and yet the depression deepened during his presidency. Claude Pepper queried, "If letting business run the country . . . is the panacea for . . . prosperity, why did we have the depression of 1929? There was nothing at that time for business to be afraid of. They did not have the governmental jitters then."[14] William Borah declared, "this depression began . . . when confidence was at its height."[15] Senator James Murray noted in 1938 that clearly "there was no . . . lack of confidence . . . during 1935 and 1936," for industry made great profits in those years.[16]

New Dealers and progressives further related their critique of confidence to the purchasing power thesis. The real problem, they argued, lay in the lack of mass buying power. Without such buying power no amount of "confidence" would renew the economy; businessmen would not invest to produce that which could not be consumed; the difficulty was economic not psychological. Give business customers, and confidence would reappear automatically; investment would follow; and prosperity would return. Senators Alben Barkley, Lewis Schwellenbach, and Theodore Francis Green all argued along these lines.[17] "The 'confidence' of investors is not undermined by politics, taxes, or banking difficulties," Phil La Follette concluded. "The . . . lack of confidence . . . is the lack of balance between capacity to produce and ability to consume."[18]

The basic theory which tied together conservatives of all varieties, and which underlay the conservative stance on a wide array of specific issues, was the confidence-natural recovery thesis, itself based upon the assumptions of classical economics. The key was confidence; from this investment flowed; and upon investment all else—production, employment, wages, consumption—depended. Essentially a conservative argument, the thesis was not without impact among bonafide radicals—witness Norman Thomas. (But Socialist Thomas, of course, gave the thesis a different twist. While conservatives used it to denounce New Deal tinkering as destructive of capitalism and recovery, Thomas used it to illustrate the fragility of capitalism and the futility of trying to reform or regulate it along New Deal-progressive lines.)

New Deal-progressive critics of the confidence thesis proceeded from three main points. Some insisted that customers came before confidence, that the real problem was lack of mass purchasing power. Restore buying power, create a market for the goods of industry, and confidence would quickly reappear. Others attacked the thesis on the related grounds afforded by the mature economy thesis. The lack of "confidence," they argued, was now inherent in the system quite apart from government policies; there simply was no longer enough real inducement for private capital investment. Others simply pointed out that if confidence was the key there should have been no depression in 1929, when a probusiness administration was in power, nor should the depression have deepened under the friendly auspices of the Hoover regime in 1930–32.

THE PURCHASING POWER THESIS

The purchasing power thesis was intellectually rooted in underconsumptionist economic theory; it further flowed from traditional progressive concerns about the nation's chronic maldistribution of wealth (and even from the mass consumption concepts of American business). The thesis cohered with its depression context: did not too much money exist in the form of capital—now,* necessarily, idle capital—and too little in the form of mass buying power? If "overproduction" existed, was this not because of the maldistribution of wealth? Moreover, the idea of economic maturity, the vogue of economic nationalism, and the shrinkage of American exports, provided further bases for the thesis; all could lead men to argue that the remedy lay in an expanding domestic market for the products of American enterprise. Like the confidence thesis, the purchasing power thesis was linked to both abstract theory and specific programs, and it ran like an iron rod through these years of depression.

The purchasing power thesis was the New Deal-progressive equivalent of the conservatives' confidence thesis. Each was widely espoused; each was considered crucial by its adherents. The

purchasing power thesis was the economic argument that united
the New Deal-progressive group; it was the analysis advanced by
most of them to explain the depression's cause and to provide
for its cure; and it complemented other New Deal-progressive
themes. Like the confidence thesis, it was part and parcel of the
larger "reform versus recovery" debate of the day. Where conservatives argued that reforms would impede recovery, New
Dealers and progressives replied that reforms were recovery's very
prerequisites. The purchasing power thesis thus provided an economic rationale for the whole host of New Deal measures aimed
at social welfare.

The inequitable distribution of purchasing power lay behind
the depression, the thesis ran; consumptive capacity had failed
to keep up with productive capacity, resulting in "overproduction," lessened employment, falling demand, and a downward
spiral. The key to recovery was increased mass purchasing power;
to provide that purchasing power a more equitable distribution
of income was needed, a larger share going to wages, and a
lesser share to profits. Higher wages, shorter hours, lower prices,
farm programs, unemployment insurance, old age pensions, and
graduated taxation were among the means suggested to redistribute income and augment purchasing power. Proponents of the
thesis often warned, when recovery seemed on the rise, especially
in 1935, 1936, and early 1937, that the boom would prove artificial
and collapse unless sustained by a firm foundation of buying
power. When the recession broke in 1937, many ascribed it to
just such a lack of buying power.

Such New Dealers and progressives as Harry Hopkins,
Henry Wallace, Frank Murphy, and Phil La Follette all espoused
the thesis. "I'm committed . . . to the purchasing-power theory
and belief in . . . better distribution of income," Hopkins declared. "The measures with which this administration chose to
fight depression were mainly directed toward one central . . .
purpose. That was to fortify consumer purchasing power."[19]
Wallace maintained that the crucial need was redistribution of
the national income to balance consumption and production. "For
the moment," he wrote in late 1936, "agriculture has no protection against another overproduction crisis." But this was true "of

our economy as a whole. . . . Production outruns consumption. We have developed no remedy."[20] "The key to the question," said Murphy, ". . . is in the redistribution of the purchasing power of the people."[21] "There is no alternative," La Follette stressed, "to conscious distribution of income."[22]

Senator Robert Wagner placed "the failure of purchasing power at the center of all explanations of depression. . . ."[23] He saw in the maldistribution of income the depression's source, and in its redistribution the depression's remedy. He therefore regarded higher wages, a shorter work week, unemployment insurance, and old age pensions as economic as well as social imperatives. A student of unemployment before the crash, Wagner repeatedly argued that the recovery of business had advanced beyond recovery in terms of reemployment and real wages, and that, if continued, the business boom would collapse. Profits and wages had not been realigned, he lamented; profits could not be reinvested because purchasing power was too low and prices were too high for increased production to be absorbed.[24]

Franklin Roosevelt also adhered to the thesis. "The first task of industry," he declared, was to provide buying power. "Only thus can we continue recovery and restore the balance we seek."[25] The fundamental problem was lack of mass purchasing power. The need was for a greater national income, more widely distributed. That one-third of a nation lacking adequate buying power had to be given its share. Higher wages and shorter hours were means to this end, the President thought, as well as programs to boost farm buying power, and social security and unemployment insurance laws to cushion the economy. Like Wagner, Roosevelt expressed concern over the slow recovery in reemployment and payrolls as compared to production.[26]

Socialist Norman Thomas endorsed the essentials of the thesis.[27] To be successful "even on its own terms," he wrote in 1933, "the New Deal must give us rapidly . . . a more direct attack on the redistribution of income through . . . unemployment relief and public works, higher wages, a drastic revision of taxation, and social insurance."[28] But recovery did not bring comparable reemployment; the New Deal did not basically confront or deal with the imperative need for income redistribution.[29] "Theoretically," Thomas concluded, "the Roosevelt Administration recognized [the problem] . . . and set about . . . increasing consumers' demands. This meant increase of purchasing power for the masses and a shift in the distribution of . . . national income." However, "the Roosevelt Administration did not put into effect, or at least did not put into effect with sufficient force, the steps necessary to increase effectively the purchasing power of the masses."[30]

Other proponents of the purchasing power thesis included progressives Bob La Follette, La Guardia, Borah, and Burton Wheeler, and New Dealers Black, Maverick, Mead, and Earle.[31] The thesis thus joined together New Dealers, progressives, and radicals, though radicals questioned whether it could be implemented under capitalism, and various of its proponents lamented through the thirties its lack of adequate implementation. "Every man on the street corner will tell you that the depression has come because our consuming power did not equal our productive output," Bronson Cutting declared, "yet practically no one acts as if this were so."[32] The New Deal, Congressman Jerry Voorhis concluded in his autobiography, "never developed an effective . . . answer to the central problem with which it sought to deal," the need to equate consumptive with productive capacity.[33]

The purchasing power thesis was the central New Deal-progressive explanation of the depression; it provided an economic rationale for New Deal programs designed to aid workers and farmers; and it neatly coincided with the New Deal's basis of support in the "Roosevelt Coalition." Many of its proponents, moreover, stressed that the potential for expanded consumption was enormous, that if workers, farmers, and the underprivileged could be given adequate purchasing power, "overproduction" would cease to exist. Critics of the thesis from the right argued that its proponents misconceived the nature of the economic process; commentators from the left suggested that something more fundamental than a New Deal-progressive socioeconomic program was needed to meet the crisis of capitalism.

Proponents of the purchasing power thesis, including, of

course, many New Dealers, were frustrated through the decade by the failure (as they saw it) of the Roosevelt administration to institutionalize the thesis. Efforts were made in that direction, they realized—there were the AAA, the NRA, the Wagner Act, wage-and-hour legislation, and so on—yet the effort never seemed to be enough. The New Deal, many of them thought, never really resolved this basic problem of income maldistribution, this fundamental malady which lay behind the failure to equate consumptive with productive capacity, this critical flaw in the economy which (in their view) was the reason for reliance upon such "palliatives" as pump priming, and the underlying cause for venturing forth into destructive phenomena to defeat depression —such as foreign loans and foreign wars.

THE EXPORTS CURE

Prospects for revived world trade seemed dim in the thirties. Throughout the world economic nationalism was in vogue, and America's foreign trade had dwindled. Some responded by arguing for an expanded domestic market to replace those markets lost abroad, for a domestic alternative to the search for extensive foreign markets. Others conceded a need to develop domestic alternatives for the "emergency"—still seeing in exports expansion the permanent solution. For the call for exports expansion was deeply rooted in the American past, and the pull of ideological—and party—tradition proved strong. Somewhat muted in the thirties, the call nonetheless persisted, a striking phenomenon in a decade that seemed to so many to be so little conducive to foreign trade expansion.

The exports cure was propounded as *the* solution to the depression by its hard-core proponents such as Secretary of State Cordell Hull. It was especially appealing to those Democrats who were neither firm conservatives nor firm New Dealers, and who were thus neither firm proponents of the confidence thesis or the purchasing power thesis. To such middling Democrats, it was attractive both as traditional party dogma and as an alternative to economic planning. The exports cure was supported by some conservative Democrats who also propounded the confidence thesis, and it tempted various New Deal Democrats who advanced the purchasing power thesis. The exports remedy also derived from the interests of those segments of the economy—such as southern cotton—long dependent for prosperity upon foreign outlets, and it found practical expression in Hull's reciprocity program passed in 1934.

Democrats often focused their criticisms upon the Republican foreign economic policies of the twenties and the Smoot-Hawley tariff of 1930. The policies of the twenties, they argued, had failed to adjust to America's new status as a creditor nation, and had created an artificial prosperity by financing exports through loans. The Smoot-Hawley tariff, they held, intensified (or even "caused") the depression by provoking retaliatory tariffs and aggravating economic nationalism abroad, thereby destroying much of America's vital export trade. As Maryland's Senator Millard Tydings put it, "we would have had the depression in 1921 . . . had it not been that we were making loans to our customers with which they were buying our goods, and the minute we stopped making those loans the whole economic fabric crashed."[34]

The export cure's central point was that prosperity at home depended upon exports abroad, that the surplus produced at home had to be exported or the depression would continue. Reciprocal trade, proponents contended, afforded the means to this end. Kentucky Senator M. M. Logan, for example, declared that "to relieve unemployment we had better join with men like . . . Hull . . . to . . . find . . . markets in which to sell the products of our farms and . . . factories."[35] Missouri Senator Bennett Champ Clark called for reciprocal trade legislation in order "to dispose of our surpluses, the sale of which has led the way out of every depression which this country has . . . known. . . ."[36] Pat Harrison and Robert Doughton, spokesmen in Congress for the reciprocity program, insisted that the ten per cent export outlet could be the "balance wheel or 'margin of safety'" for the nation's economy.[37]

New Deal Democrats, while espousing the purchasing power thesis, also tended to place a traditional emphasis on the export trade. Franklin Roosevelt, for example, while lacking Hull's dogmatism, flexible on the issue, open to experimentation with alternatives early in his administration, and unable to see in foreign trade *the* path to recovery, nonetheless frequently called for the reestablishment of foreign markets. FDR declared that "The full reward of America's high productive capacity is only gained when our business men and our farmers can sell their surpluses abroad. This is true of every great surplus-producing Nation." Foreign trade restoration was the only way the nation could avoid agonizing dislocations and unemployment.[38]

New Dealer Henry Wallace argued that a continued shrinkage of the export trade would result in a "regimented" domestic economy and that such "regimentation" would end in autocracy. He argued in his 1934 pamphlet *America Must Choose* that an isolated path would require "a . . . regimentation of agriculture and industry far beyond that which anyone has yet suggested." It would "mean the shifting of millions of people from the farms of the South. . . . [It would require] the extraordinarily complete control of all the agencies of public opinion . . . necessary to carry through a program of isolated prosperity."[39] Conservative Democrat Lewis Douglas agreed. Economic isolation, he held, was not possible in a free society. It required regimentation by government. It would impoverish the South, the cornbelt, and the export-producing industrial regions. The ensuing dislocations would require production restriction and ever-increasing degrees of government control, leading finally to a collectivist state.[40]

Finally, some Republicans charged that for all their ridicule of the foreign loans of the twenties, the New Deal Democrats were following essentially similar policies. John Taber, for example, contended that through American purchases of foreign silver "we get ourselves in just the same position that we got into between 1920 and 1929, when we sold our goods to foreign countries and took back . . . bonds. It is just the same process."[41] Hamilton Fish, recalling that FDR in 1932 had attacked loans abroad to finance exports, charged that the New Deal's Export-Import Bank was designed to do this very thing.[42] (Congressman Fish, however, advanced a similar proposal. He noted the difficulties involved in selling products to countries which lacked, as most did, a sufficient gold supply to pay for them. He denied that reciprocal trade provided the solution because it would only cause domestic unemployment. "I am not saying right now that we should loan . . . money to other nations," he concluded, "but I am not so sure that we should not put aside $1,000,000,000 . . . of gold as a revolving fund for those nations that need our cotton—Japan, Germany, and Italy. . . .")[43]   •

The case for the exports cure began with a critique of the policies of the twenties: foreign loans to finance exports, high tariffs (culminating in Smoot-Hawley), and the failure to adjust policy to America's postwar status as a creditor nation resulted first in a period of artificial prosperity, then in retaliatory tariffs, a world trend toward closed economic systems, the decline of the American export trade, mounting surpluses, unemployment, and depression. The cure stressed the dependence of domestic prosperity upon foreign trade: many commodities (cotton was a key example) had long been dependent upon export markets for an outlet. The argument was thus commodity-based; it was also traditional Democratic party doctrine, especially popular in the South. Some leaders saw in expanded trade *the* solution to depression, and espoused the exports cure dogmatically; others were attracted by it, especially given the argument that a lost export trade would result in internal "regimentation."

This antiregimentation and antiplanning corollary was key. Along with their traditional party concepts, it made the exports cure appealing to middling Democrats uneasy about the New Deal. It was also appealing to such conservative Democrats as Lewis Douglas and to such New Dealers as Henry Wallace, both of whom saw it as an alternative to their version of a regimented domestic economy. The antiregimentation, antiplanning corollary was thus an illustration in a foreign economic policy context of the dogmatic mode of thinking found in the conservatives' view of the New Deal's ultimate logic and consequences, and in the New Dealers' view of the ultimate logic and consequences of programs more radical than their own. Critics used the term "regimentation" to describe the New Deal's intervention; New Dealers used it to describe alternatives more radical than their own.

The idea of artificial prosperity appeared not only in the

Democratic critique of the loans of the twenties but also in the Taber-Fish criticisms of the New Deal's allegedly analogous devices. Fish's comment that such a stratagem should perhaps be tried again, moreover, in the form of a "revolving fund," showed the continuing temptation of such an "easy" remedy. Finally, the New Deal Democrats' attraction to the exports cure, even as they advanced the purchasing power thesis, implicitly called into question the New Deal's own ability to construct a genuine prosperity based upon permanent rearrangements rather than an artificial one based upon continually contrived expedients. It once again evidenced an overall New Deal pattern and syndrome: the tension between the purchasing power thesis and the unwillingness to depart too far from the bounds of traditional orthodoxies, the inability to implement analyses when potential programs transcended traditional dogmas.

THE MONEY CURE

Another remedy, with roots deep in America's past, looked to monetary formulae to resolve the depression. As the crisis deepened, so, too, did the cry for the money cure; it reached a pitch in 1933, declined as recovery advanced at mid-decade, and revived briefly during the recession of 1937–38.[44] Essentially southern and western, rural and agricultural, it was armed with the ethos and ideology of Bryanism. Its adherents characteristically argued that the "money question" was the key question, the resolution of which would lead the way to recovery. They usually propounded the "quantitative theory of money," the idea that an expansion of the currency would cheapen money, raise prices, ease debts, and ensure recovery, as the underlying rationale for their particular proposals. And they often insisted that such "expedients" as the NRA and the AAA would not be needed if inflation were adopted, looking to currency expansion (as others looked to exports expansion) as an alternative to economic planning.

Elmer Thomas, Oklahoma Senator and veteran of the Bryan campaigns of 1896 and 1900, was a money man par excellence. His doctrines were long-held; he expressed the spirit of '96 steadfastly, dogmatically, and very frequently. Considering the "money question" crucial, he contended that the need was to place more money in circulation, making it plentiful, making it cheaper, and thereby raising prices. The law of supply and demand applied to money as well as to other commodities; when money was plentiful, it was cheap, prices were high, and times were good; contraction brought deflation and hard times. If enough money were placed in circulation, Thomas stressed, there would be no need for production restriction plans; prices would rise automatically. Such recovery as occurred he ascribed to administration monetary measures.[45]

Congressmen Wright Patman and John Rankin were likewise two of the decade's most persistent proponents of the monetary cure. Patman consistently emphasized the need for currency expansion. Money had been made scarce, he argued, and therefore wages and prices had fallen. Expand the currency and prices and wages would rise and farmers' debts would be more easily paid. With the money cure, "the depression will be over, and all temporary expedients may be immediately repealed. . . ."[46] Rankin argued that currency expansion was the only way out of the depression. It would raise commodity prices, restore purchasing power, and spur agricultural and general recovery. The depression was a "money panic." Currency expansion was key; all "expedients" were secondary. With currency expansion, "you would not need the N.R.A., . . . artificial stimulation," or farm production controls.[47]

The money cure, some suggested, could best be implemented through silver. The momentum of silverism rose during the early thirties; its influence, like that of the money movement generally, was greatest during the depression's peak of intensity;[48] and its roots likewise lay deep in American history. Some of its leading spokesmen had been imbued with the ideology of the white metal during the nineties,[49] and to such men it was an age-old verity vindicated by the crisis of the thirties. Along with the idea that silver formulae would implement the familiar quantitative theory, thus expanding the currency, raising prices, facilitating debt payment, and speeding recovery, many silverites argued that by increasing the purchasing power of the silver-using countries great new export markets for the United States would be opened up in Latin America and the Orient—thereby solving the "surplus" problem without resort to such domestic programs as production restriction.

The inflationary quest clearly had roots in economic conditions and interests. The demand for inflation was a traditional agrarian response to hard times; the money men spoke for farm interests and were products of an agricultural milieu. The specific demand that something be done for silver, moreover, was rooted in the economic interests of the mining states of the West and proponents of silver, inflation, and farm aid were often sympathetic allies with intertwined objectives. But the drive for currency expansion derived from political traditions as well as economic conditions; to its proponents, the money cure was not only an economic program but also an article of faith. Wright Patman, Elmer Thomas, and William Lemke all gave the New Deal general support while bemoaning its failure to come to grips with what they considered the central—the monetary—problem.[50] Resolve the money problem, such men declared, and the need for the New Deal's "expedients" would soon cease to exist.

In their aversion to production controls the money men were akin to the natural recovery conservatives and to many of those who stressed export trade expansion—thus further evidencing the persistence of the "antiplanning" strain. This could make monetary formulae, like the exports cure, attractive to middling Democrats uneasy about the New Deal's planning, and also to such "antibureaucratic" progressives as Borah, Wheeler, and Gerald Nye. Moreover, the argument that great new markets for America would be opened up by increasing the purchasing power of silver-using countries further showed how money men and export trade enthusiasts could join forces: doing something for silver would expand exports, and do it without expanding "bureaucracy." Like the exports cure, then, monetary formulae could appeal to those who also looked elsewhere for depression remedies; the money cure's influence spread beyond its hard-core proponents.[51] Like the exports cure, it would provide an "easy" way out of hard times.

THE 1937-38 RECESSION

The 1937–38 recession lent new urgency to the ongoing depression debate; the broad contours of the larger debate remained, but the new context modified some of the specific applications; the recession debate thus reflected both basic and altered ideas about the depression, and the adjustment of continuing concepts to new conditions. Conservatives, for example, argued that the recession was "political," caused by unsound government policies. This analysis proceeded from the confidence thesis; a corollary held that while the depression of "1929–32" had been worldwide, the "new depression" was distinctly domestic in origin. The policies most often criticized in this connection, as in the confidence thesis per se, included monetary tinkering, deficit spending, undue taxation, and harassment of business, to which were added uncertainty over administration policies, and sit-down strikes. The recession, conservatives concluded, validated their 1933–36 argument that the New Deal had retarded the natural upswing of recovery.

This explanation was widely espoused. Arthur Vandenberg, for example, argued that "The policies of government are responsible for what has happened, and only a change in the policies of government can correct the dangerous drift."[52] Senator Styles Bridges contended that the recession was "Government made, and therefore . . . can be corrected by action of the Government."[53] Bertrand Snell held that the recession, unlike the depression, was domestic and not worldwide; its source lay in New Deal policies; it sprang "from political, not economic causes. It can be cured only by political action. . . ."[54] Frank Knox argued that New Deal policies provoked the crisis; "political action . . . destroyed confidence and dammed up the flow of capital."[55]

The conservatives' cardinal analysis of the recession, within the "political" recession context, centered on the New Deal's undistributed profits and capital gains taxes. These taxes, the argument went, restricted expansion, retarded recovery, and provoked recession. At a psychological level they destroyed confidence and dammed up investment; at a policy level they had a like effect, taking away from enterprise the very capital needed to renew and to reactivate the economy. The conservatives' attacks upon the taxes once again reflected their stress on the key role of private investment and the close gearing of their arguments to business interests. Those proceeding in this vein included the bipartisan authors of the "Conservative Manifesto," Republicans Bridges, Treadway, and Fish, and Democratic Senators Royal Copeland and Peter Gerry.[56]

New Dealers disputed the conservative contention that taxes triggered the recession. In so doing, they repeated much of their critique of the confidence thesis. Alben Barkley, for example, insisted that these taxes "did not deter capital expansion. . . . During the first 6 months of 1937, when both . . . taxes were in fullest effect, we had as much plant expansion as in the halcyon days of 1928."[57] Senator James Pope declared that the taxes "were imposed for the purpose of preventing precisely what happened in 1937."[58] New Dealers thus rejected the conservatives' critique of the New Deal's tax policies, and with it the conservatives' "political" explanation of the recession. They in turn fashioned alternative explanations, reflecting their own continuing and changing conceptions of the economic crisis.

A major New Deal analysis utilized the administered prices concept, the idea that powerful corporations controlled their own prices. A favorite of New Dealers in explaining the 1937–38 recession, this essential idea had been persistently propounded by such progressives as Burt Wheeler and William Borah for years; it was an orthodox antimonopoly argument refashioned into one of the New Deal's key concepts; it brought progressive thinking circa 1933 into the mainstream of New Deal ideology circa 1938. As Franklin Roosevelt expressed it, "One of the things . . . that brought on the . . . recession . . . was the fact that some things . . . went clear through the roof and people quit buying."[59] Congressman Robert G. Allen added that big businesses hiked "prices to such an extent . . . that people could not buy back the very goods which they made. . . ."[60]

New Dealers also focused on the 1937 cutback in federal spending. George Earle, for example, declared that "President Roosevelt made big business pay big taxes and created purchasing power among the masses, and the depression was stopped.

As soon as government spending was curtailed the cycle went down."[61] Franklin Roosevelt contended that pump priming had brought recovery, and that the recession resulted in part from the failure of business to take up the slack resulting from the reduction in federal spending.[62] Robert Wagner argued that federal spending spurred recovery from 1933 to 1937; "It was only when the Federal Government . . . cut down its contributions to purchasing power," he asserted, ". . . that there . . . began the sharp decline of business."[63]

Many combined the two explanations. Fiorello La Guardia, for example, credited the recovery to public works spending; the problem was that "business . . . missed the ball." The spending was designed to spur recovery; business should have "cooperated" with government in this endeavor by keeping prices down. Had this been done, the recession would not have resulted when the spending stopped.[64] James Murray, like La Guardia, argued that pump priming had revived prosperity, and that industry had failed to cooperate with government by taking up the slack in spending. Instead of maintaining purchasing power through high wages and low prices, industry hiked prices inordinately.[65] Maury Maverick, too, ascribed the recession to inordinate administered prices, and to the failure of business to take up the slack in public spending.[66]

Norman Thomas presented a socialist version of the recession, which, however, consisted in good part of a medley of conservative and New Deal themes within the radical context. He argued that the crisis was inherent in a capitalist system no longer expanding (that it was, in this sense, a symptom of the larger malady), and that it was also and more immediately due to lack of confidence, the cutback in federal spending, and high administered prices in the capital goods industries. Arguing that the recession was inherent in the system, he denied that it was the work of "wicked men." Moreover, he asserted, the "recession was no more due to the New Deal's tax policy or to its regulation of the stock market than to . . . [a] capitalist plot."[67]

Finally there were those who argued that the recession had monetary roots, a reflection of one of the most persistent of all explanations of economic crisis. Mississippi Democrat John

Rankin, long an advocate of monetary remedies, focused on the Chairman of the Federal Reserve Board, declaring that "the one man most responsible for this recession is probably Mr. Marriner S. Eccles. . . . This recession is caused by a contraction of the currency. . . ."[68] Texas Democrat Wright Patman asserted that "Mr. Marriner S. Eccles . . . caused this recession when he and the . . . Governors of the Federal Reserve Board increased . . . the reserve requirements of the banks."[69] North Dakota Congressman Usher Burdick and Senator Elmer Thomas also argued along these lines.[70]

The debate over the recession reflected in microcosm many of the general attitudes toward depression and recovery expressed through the decade. Conservatives, for example, based their particular arguments upon the confidence thesis; New Dealers based their particular arguments upon the purchasing power thesis. The debate was also intriguing because of what it failed to reflect. Unlike the earlier debate over the crisis of 1929–33, some crucial ingredients were seldom to be found. Although farm policy and foreign economic policy were discussed at length in the earlier debate over the depression's origins, they were seldom focused upon as key causal agents in this one. Instead of a central role for agriculture, labor—in the debate over the sit-down strikes—entered into the discussion, perhaps reflecting the increasingly important role of unions in political concern by the later thirties.

The debate further showed how the conservatives could adjust their confidence thesis to fit the twists and turns of economic realities. While the depression of 1929–32 had been worldwide, the argument went, this one was distinctly domestic in origin; while the earlier depression represented the whirlwind of the World War, the present one had no such source; while the earlier depression had not been inherent in the American system, this one was inherent in the New Deal's tinkering with that system; while the earlier depression had been on the wane in 1932, this new one was the inevitable outcome of the New Deal's check of that "natural" upward trend. Among radicals, the recession further confirmed their thesis that capitalism had lost its dynamic, and that a New Deal could not, in the long run, restore that dynamic. Among monetary reformers, too, the recession confirmed a long-time analysis: the money problem was key, they argued, and it was no less crucial in 1938 than in 1933.

Among New Dealers, the recession debate showed their increasing stress upon two phenomena within the context of their long-time purchasing power thesis: the efficacy of public spending and the adverse impact of "administered" monopoly prices. The recession debate put spending at the core of the discussion; it became the central program for New Dealers to support and to defend: no longer were there the complexities of the NRA, no longer schemes to plan the economy, but the external stimulus of spending in a period in which the radical and epochal mood of 1933 had given way to a more conservative and traditionalist bent. The stress on spending and monopoly by New Dealers reflected this new mood: spending utilized traditional techniques of government—the Supreme Court was hardly likely to declare deficits unconstitutional—and "monopoly" was one of the oldest and most hated of all American ogres.

THE FISCAL EXPEDIENT

Fiscal policy has become closely associated with the thirties; John Maynard Keynes's *General Theory of Employment, Interest and Money* was published in 1936. But Keynesian ideas were at most on the very fringes of the political debate. The idea of spending to spur recovery was a common one, yet few held it to be *the* answer to depression. Indeed most spenders simultaneously espoused other programs which they regarded as more "fundamental" than mere "pump priming." Spending was initially employed as a stopgap, as a complement to the more grandiose schemes of 1933–35; and it was cut back in 1937 when a measure of "recovery" seemingly had been achieved. After the recession broke it was—with much hesitation—revitalized; but even though it had by mid-1938 become more than any other *the* administration recovery program, it was still rationalized as a crisis expedient.

For New Dealers and like-minded progressives remained fundamentally fearful, uneasy, and ambivalent about spending. They expressed qualms, characterized it as a "palliative," and regarded it as an emergency device. Even supporters of the "cyclical" idea fretted about the seemingly interminable length of the downward (and hence the spending) cycle of the thirties. Robert Wagner, for example, stressed in 1935 that government spending should be reduced once business was fully revived. Public works do prime the pump, he added in 1936, "But priming cannot go on forever."[71] Henry Wallace focused on the need for private industry to take over once public funds had slackened, warning that a budget too long unbalanced would end in inflation and economic "disaster."[72] Fiorello La Guardia declared of public works and federal spending, "even those are palliatives. . . . Machinery is displacing labor all . . . the time."[73]

Conservative critics of pump priming often conceded that spending brought prosperity; but they contended that it was prosperity of an "artificial," ephemeral, and non-self-sustaining sort. Allen Treadway, for example, asserted in 1936 that "a large part of the present recovery is artificial, being based on the New Deal's . . . spending. . . ."[74] L. J. Dickinson denied that "temporary relief, provided through . . . government funds . . . , has brought about [any] permanent solution. . . . These enormous expenditures . . . provided merely temporary stimulants, like the administration of a drug. . . ."[75] And Arthur Vandenberg similarly warned that spending, "like any other artificial recourse, cannot be an interminable operation. . . . Hypodermics are good as stimulants; fatal as a prolonged reliance. . . ."[76]

Public spending was sharply criticized by conservatives on more rigid, dogmatic, ideologically abstract grounds as well; it was, given their philosophical assumptions, a reckless departure from tested fiscal policy. Relating their critique to the confidence thesis, they charged that excessive and deficit spending imperiled the nation's credit, threatened inflation, frightened business, drained away private capital, hampered private investment, and retarded genuine recovery. In short, it disrupted the economy's vital processes, preventing the normal functioning of the system. Among those denouncing public spending in such terms and (or) demanding a return to fiscal orthodoxy were Democrats Byrd, Bailey, Carter Glass, and Lewis Douglas, and Republicans Hoover, Mills, Landon, and Knox.[77]

As recovery progressed, from 1935 into 1937, the cry went up that the emergency was over, that good times were on the way, and that a return to fiscal orthodoxy was therefore in order. South Carolina's James Byrnes, for example, asserted in June 1937 that "recovery has taken place." "If in times such as now exist . . . we cannot reduce the indebtedness incurred during the emergency—if we cannot even live within our income—I ask . . . , when can we . . . do it?"[78] Not only middling Democrats, however, but also New Dealers could sound this theme. The New Deal camp was in fact split over this issue, reflecting thereby its inner ambivalence over spending. Its adherents agreed that spending was an emergency measure, but when was the "emergency" over? Was it over with the partial recovery of 1936? Was the "cycle" now sufficiently on the upswing? Or did the millions yet unemployed suggest otherwise?

The 1937–38 recession sparked a more intense—and in the depression controversy as a whole, an ever more central—debate over public spending. The recession, of course, added new urgency to the conservative cry that the New Deal stood in the way of recovery, and that its fiscal policies could not bring sound and lasting prosperity. GOP National Chairman John D. M. Hamilton, for example, boasted, "We warned that New Deal prosperity was a house of cards which could not stand unless constantly supported by government spending."[79] Alf Landon fretted, "If every time there is a recession . . . the only way out that . . . government can find is a . . . huge expenditure program . . . , then we shall go bankrupt."[80] And Allen Treadway held that pump priming would do no more than spur another "artificial recovery," doomed again to collapse when the spending stopped.[81]

Supporters of the New Deal, on the other hand, backed renewed spending to meet the recession, but again looked to it only for the "emergency," looking elsewhere for more permanent formulae to implement the purchasing power thesis. The "permanent" solution, many suggested, lay in antimonopoly. Senator Theodore Francis Green, for example, argued that while spending spurred the economy it was but a stopgap, and "no permanent cure. The permanent cure must take other forms," such as reducing working hours, and "beating down" high monopoly prices.[82] James Murray agreed that public spending had induced the recovery of the mid-thirties, and that it was needed to induce recovery again. But the new spending program, he stressed, was "not intended in itself as a solution of our economic problems." A "permanent cure" required a different course, including an end to monopoly, and a wider distribution of income.[83] And Maury Maverick supported the 1938 spending program, while arguing that it would "not . . . settle the depression." The crucial problem, he suggested, lay in "the failure of the Government to regulate monopoly, own it, or destroy it. . . ."[84]

Most supporters conceived of spending in temporary pump priming rather than in Keynesian or (to use the administration's leading spokesman for a more permanent fiscal cure) Marriner Eccles's terms. They had qualms as to spending's efficacy and arrived at even the pump priming position reluctantly. They saw it as an emergency stimulus that could be removed once business had revived—a position reflected in their criticism of business for not taking up the slack occasioned by the government's curtailment of spending in 1937. They often conceded that spending was merely a "palliative," a stopgap; that it was less "fundamental" than other programs, failing to go to the root of the malady; that other programs would truly institute the purchasing power thesis rather than merely expand buying power on an "emergency" basis.

The conservatives' critique of spending held that pump priming resulted in an "artificial," non-self-sustaining prosperity that would cease to exist when the spending which created and sustained it ceased to flow. Invoking their omnipresent confidence thesis, conservatives saw spending as the very preventive of permanent recovery: deficit finance and excessive taxation undermined confidence, hence investment, hence self-sustaining prosperity. Their critique of spending was also related to their view of the depression's origins. Depressions had been ended before without massive spending, they argued; why not now? This de-

pression was basically like earlier depressions; why did the remedies have to differ? Thus the conservative critique of spending
wholly cohered with both the conservative confidence thesis and
the conservative view of the depression's origins and the way to
recovery.

While some argued after mid-decade that with a return to
good times fiscal orthodoxy was in order, and that with the
emergency over, emergency expedients should be scrapped; the
ambivalence of New Dealers over spending was reflected in their
divisions over this issue: some—though not others—were willing
and anxious to retrench by 1937. President Roosevelt's spending
cutback in that year, and the opposition to it of some New Dealers, was illustrative of this division within the proadministration
camp. Moreover, the rationale expressed by New Dealers in their
support of the 1938 resumption of spending—that it was an
"emergency" measure, that more "permanent" cures would have
to be found elsewhere (in antimonopolism, for example)—
showed that even at this point the fiscal remedy was still looked
upon in short-range pump priming rather than in long-range
Keynesian terms.

The debate over spending in 1938 was a culmination of the
five years of controversy. For supporters, in whose ideas spending
by 1938 had come to play a central role, the recession proved the
need for renewed spending. Spending had induced recovery, they
argued; when it was curtailed, the recession broke; now it was
needed to induce recovery again. For conservative critics of
spending, the recession proved everything that they had said
about pump priming: that it could produce only an artificial
prosperity, that the recovery induced by spending would collapse
when the spending stopped, that spending prevented "natural"
recovery from taking place, that another pump priming program
would only repeat the pattern of 1933–37—artificial revival,
spending cuts, boom to bust.

4

FARM POLICY

Farm policy discussion reflected many of the characteristics of the overall debate and provided some further twists.
The antiplanning theme again appeared, concepts of economic
interdependence were presented, and the concept of "balance"
was at the core of much of the controversy. The specific debate
over crop control evidenced a multiplicity of general themes: the
emergency rationale, the idea of a "norm," the critique of
scarcity economics, the critique of the planning philosophy, and
differing concepts of "regimentation." The Agricultural Adjustment Administration was designed to help implement the purchasing power thesis, and this provided a further focus. Like NRA, the
"middle way" nature of the AAA attracted much opposition
from both left and right. It could be opposed on the right on the
grounds of classical economy, and on the left—ironically—on the
grounds of the purchasing power thesis. For the AAA, like the
NRA, illustrated the difficulties and dilemmas inherent in the
New Dealers' limited attempts to implement the purchasing
power thesis. What was done to implement the thesis in one sector of the economy could be undone by the attempt to implement
the thesis in another, and both efforts could in turn be stymied
by the power of private corporations. Alternatives presented to
crop control showed the persistence of traditional formulae, as

well as some further potential applications of the purchasing
power thesis.

CRISIS

The farm economy in 1933 was in a state of severe crisis.
The agricultural depression had existed through the twenties; with
the general collapse agriculture sank deeper into the morass. The
decline in foreign trade after 1929, and the decrease in domestic
capacity to consume, left farmers with mounting surpluses, falling prices, and shrinking incomes. The post-1929 crisis also found
farmers' representatives equipped with certain assumptions about
the role of agriculture in the economy, assumptions shaped by
agriculture's decade-long depression. One such assumption was
that the agricultural depression of the twenties was a (or the)
major cause of the general depression. The paucity of farm purchasing power, the argument went, reduced the market for the
products of industry, thereby ending in urban as well as rural
collapse. Many contended, as the other side of this coin, that
restoration of farm prosperity was the sine qua non of industrial
and general recovery.

Concern over agriculture's inadequate buying power, moreover, could cause "emergency" and "artificiality" concepts to be
intermeshed in a curious way. Josiah Bailey, for example, that
otherwise stanch foe of artificial schemes, declared that "so long
as farmers, constituting 27 percent of the . . . population, receive
only 10 percent of the national income, we are justified in involving artificial measures to bring up the price to the farmers.
. . ."[1] Gerald Nye and Hatton Sumners both provided more representative examples of the aversion of American political leaders
to "artificial" devices, looking to agricultural recovery (as some
looked to currency expansion or to an exports revival) to obviate
any need for such "expedients." Senator Nye suggested that with
farm "buying power restored there will be far less need for
artificial methods of getting men back to work in . . . factories.
. . ."[2] Texas Congressman Sumners asserted, "if we could revive
the buying power of the farmers, and possibly, under necessity,

reduce the dollar, we would not have to have all these alphabets under which we are working."[3]

Others placed their plea for increased farm purchasing power within the conceptual framework of the interdependence of farmers and industrial workers, of farm and industrial prosperity, of each group upon the other as a market for its products. But the concept of economic interdependence came in several versions, and it could be used as a veneer for older and more deeply rooted attitudes and beliefs. Senate majority leader Joseph Robinson, for example, conceded in 1933 that the AAA's processing tax might increase the cost of living, but added that it would be more than offset by the increased market prosperous farmers would provide for the products of industrial workers.[4] Marvin Jones, chairman of the House Committee on Agriculture, contended in 1935 that the AAA's higher farm prices had not hurt consumers, that they were "more than offset by the tremendously increased purchasing power of the farmer and his subsequent purchases of the manufactured product. . . ."[5]

William Borah dissented; and, in so doing, related the farmer's problem to that of monopoly. Asked by Senator Allen Ellender whether he agreed that crop control legislation would increase farm purchasing power and thereby speed industrial recovery, Borah responded, "that did not happen in 1929. In 1928 and 1929 the farmer had very fair prices for his products, but conditions obtained where the people were unable to buy what the farmer was producing." Ellender pointed out that in 1928–29 "the farmer got fairly good prices, but not in proportion to what he had to pay for what he needed," to which Borah rejoined: "That is what I am saying; let us take control of those who fix the prices of the things which the farmer has to buy."[6] The problem could only be met by striking at the crux of the malady and not (in the name of "economic interdependence") at its symptoms: and for Borah the crux was monopoly control.

The argument that the farm depression provoked the general collapse, and that farm recovery was therefore prerequisite to general restoration, was a common one among agriculture's political spokesmen in the early thirties. This argument could be closely related to several others, including the purchasing power thesis, the exports cure, the money cure, and the "parity" theme —the quest for "balance" among the various groups and sectors. The notion that prosperity on the farm was the underlying foundation of prosperity in the nation was sometimes advanced in the form of a lament, complete with sectional-agrarian overtones, that business and labor were profiting at agriculture's expense; but it was also often advanced as an integral part of the concept of economic interdependence—a concept that was itself, however, subject to varying emphases and interpretations.

CROP CONTROL

In the area of farm policy the stage was set before the 1929 crash. The crisis in agriculture had persisted through the twenties; accordingly, proposals for farm recovery had been debated through the decade—in the Congress, among farmers' organizations, by experts in the colleges. In the twenties the controversy centered on McNary-Haugenism and the subsidization of exports; but as the agricultural depression deepened after 1929, and as farm voices became more raucous, the emphasis shifted to more drastic remedies. In 1933—as the new administration faced an overproduction problem of crisis proportions—the evolving proposals of agricultural economists and farmers' organizations were sifted, modified, and fused by the Department of Agriculture in shaping basic policy. The central and most immediate thrust of the New Deal's attempt to meet the problem was crop control— coordinated limitation of farm production in order to reduce surpluses and thereby raise farm prices and incomes. This formula remained the administration's basic remedy through the thirties.

Yet, despite this apparent permanence, crop control was characteristically presented by its proponents as a necessary, but "temporary" and "artificial" program, to be used pending restoration of "normal" trade relations. Congressman Otha Wearin, for

example, expressed hope that conditions would improve under the
AAA "program of nationalism," but added that "a more permanent and stable prosperity" depended upon the restoration of farm
export markets. The crop control program, he declared, was "not
in harmony with the principles of the Democratic Party and is
being used . . . at the present moment as a stopgap until we can
correct such evils as were forced upon us under the Hawley-Smoot
Act. . . ."[7] Alben Barkley similarly remarked that the AAA's
"artificial methods . . . were not intended as a permanent remedy for agriculture"; they were designed for the "emergency,"
for the "artificial respiration" of agriculture until foreign trade
could be restored.[8]

The first AAA was declared unconstitutional in early 1936,
thus setting the stage for the new (or renewed) farm surplus
crisis of 1937. Franklin Roosevelt in August 1937, for example,
stressed the need for crop control if the price of cotton was to be
kept at a reasonable level. Crop control had been eliminated by
the Supreme Court; "There has been no surplus control since
then"; now the size of the cotton crop was one of the largest
ever. ". . . crop control is inevitable unless we are going to wreck
the economics of the country because every time that cotton goes
down to under ten cents or wheat below eighty cents, the purchasing power of one half the country dries up and the wheels
of the factories slow up. . . . We started in the Spring of 1933
with a perfectly good . . . program and it is going to go through."[9]
It was thus an era of "emergency" programs grown permanent;
pump priming was one, crop control another.

Advocates of crop control often pointed out that the program merely applied a long-standing business principle to the
farm, that of curtailing production to meet reduced demand. As
Franklin Roosevelt put it, "big manufacturers talk about control
of production by the farmer as an indefensible 'economy of
scarcity.' And yet these same manufacturers never hesitate to
shut down their . . . plants . . . whenever they think they must
adjust their production to an oversupply of the goods they
make."[10] William Borah, as usual, took the reasoning a step
further. Responding to Theodore Francis Green's defense of crop
control in terms of the industrial analogy, Borah declared: "I

would rather go back and make the first man [the industrialist] pursue a right course than to pursue a wrong course with reference to the second man [the farmer]. So long as private corporations fix prices you will have millions with little or no purchasing power, and so long as you have millions without purchasing power you will have a serious farm problem."[11]

A common criticism of the crop control program—and a cliché of the era—was that the real problem was underconsumption of farm products and not overproduction. Fiorello La Guardia, Norman Thomas, Upton Sinclair, and Tom Amlie, for example, all proceeded in this vein.[12] Henry Wallace, responding to such criticism, argued that "Agriculture cannot survive in a capitalistic society as a philanthropic enterprise. . . . The people who raise the cry about the last hungry Chinamen are not really criticising the farmers or the AAA, but the profit system. . . ."[13] (A Norman Thomas, if not a Fiorello La Guardia, of course, was doing precisely that.) James Pope asserted that the farmer could not produce without limit, awaiting the day when "an ideal state of affairs" would allow his surplus to be consumed by those in need of it, that he faced a crisis now. Those who criticized crop control on the ground that people were hungry and ill-clad were "merely engaged in wishful thinking and . . . contributing nothing to the solution of the farmers' problem."[14]

Some critics of crop control argued that by raising prices it served to penalize consumers and reduce consumption. Its processing tax was in effect a sales tax. It served not to create purchasing power, but to cut purchasing power in the cities, and to shift purchasing power from urban to rural areas. The decline in consumption would necessarily require further farm production restriction, and the spiral would continue downward. As New Jersey's Republican Senator Hamilton Kean put it, "the processing, or sales taxes," were drawing millions of dollars out of his state "to pay for New Deal experiments in the West and South. . . . These experiments . . . make it more expensive . . . to live, and the cost of these experiments in the high cost of living comes out of the wage-earners of New Jersey."[15] Others arguing along these lines included urban Democrats Emanuel Celler and John Mc-

Cormack, conservative Democrats Bailey and Tydings, and conservative Republicans Hoover and Mills.[16]

Norman Thomas and Jerry Voorhis,[17] as well as Hamilton Fish, Carter Glass, and William Borah, an ideologically variegated group if ever there was one, also proceeded in this vein. Fish, for example, stating his version of the theme, charged that "The Democratic Party has claimed to be the party of the consumers. . . . Now, it . . . establishes . . . processing taxes . . . which increases the cost of living to all wage earners and consumers."[18] Carter Glass, steeped in classical economics, queried, "Why should the AAA cause an artificial increase in prices? There are 130,-000,000 people who eat wheat—many more than than the number of wheat producers—and why should they suffer so as to profit a few? Everybody wears cotton. Why should we impose terrific prices on all the consumers of cotton for the sake of a comparatively small group of planters? Why should we not let the law of supply and demand operate, as it always has?"[19]

William Borah, once again, went more clearly to the crux of the matter. Through the AAA, the Idahoan contended, "We are seeking . . . to raise the price of farm commodities at the expense of the urban dweller," but the real need was to "find some method by which to increase the income of the Nation as a whole." "If a method can be found by which the purchasing power of the farmer . . . and at the same time the purchasing power of the man who buys from the farmer can be restored, we will have solved the problem of the depression."[20] The key was not to take from one group and give to the other but to expand the buying power of both. Congressman Clarence Cannon, on the other hand, stoutly denied that the AAA had made farm product prices unduly high for consumers.[21] And Senator George Norris, utilizing a version of the interdependence concept, argued that expanded farm purchasing power, increasing the market for industrial goods, offset any higher prices that workers might have to pay as consumers.[22]

A number of political leaders expressed concern about NRA's impact on agriculture, arguing that it was boosting industrial prices more rapidly than the AAA was increasing farm prices, that it was undermining the goal of parity for agriculture, and that farmers' costs of production were outrunning their incomes. This view was advanced by a wide array of leaders; among them where conservative Republicans Hoover and Fish, Socialist Norman Thomas, progressives Wheeler and Nye, conservative Democrats Tydings and Eugene Talmadge, and farm state spokesmen of both parties such as William Lemke, Peter Norbeck, John Rankin, and Clarence Cannon.[23] New Deal spokesman George McGill answered the critics, advancing another version of the interdependence concept, and arguing that the NRA, by restoring purchasing power among industrial workers, and making them better consumers, thereby indirectly benefited the nation's farmers.[24]

Conservative Republican Congressman James Wadsworth, relating the farm problem to those he considered inherent in economic planning, declared it "impossible in a country the size of the United States . . . for a central government to manage its agriculture. . . . Now see what happens when you attempt crop control. . . . The first attempt was with cotton. . . . The effect was the throwing out of occupation of thousands . . . of share croppers. . . . This had to be taken care of. How? By appropriating more money for relief. . . ." Yet "another effect . . . was that the acreage taken out of cotton was put into some other crop and that crop, in turn, had to be regulated; and when that second crop was regulated still more acreage was idle, and . . . the Congress said, 'Well, we will have to regulate that', and so on down the line until we reached potatoes. It was inevitable." "Carried to its logical conclusion, triple A must control all food crops . . . in the United States."[25]

Crop control was commonly criticized as coercive, smacking of autocracy and bureaucracy; among those pursuing this theme were Vandenberg, Mills, and Hoover.[26] As Josiah Bailey saw it, "The A.A.A. is a perfect model of fascism. . . . If we took the same act and applied it to the other activities . . . , we should have fascism, without question."[27] Ellison D. ("Cotton Ed") Smith noted the need for programs to spur recovery. "But," he added in 1933, "whether we are going to do it by turning over to the Secretary of Agriculture the entire overlordship of every farm . . . , every factory . . . , every milling process in America . . . , if that is our only hope, I am in despair."[28] The 1933 farm bill, Norman Thomas exclaimed, "will give the secretary of agriculture power no single official in Soviet Russia possesses over . . . farmers. . . ."[29] If the government can control the right to grow cotton, William Borah warned, "it is only a question of time . . . until this creeping paralysis of bureaucracy benumbs the hand of the editor."[30]

James Pope defended the New Deal farm program against the charge of "regimentation." Under the AAA, he declared, "The farmer is regimenting himself . . . to combat the solid phalanx of the industrialist with whom he does his over-the-counter dealing."[31] But some of those using the "regimentation" theme were themselves supporters of crop control. Secretary Wallace, for example, criticized proposals for stricter government control of agriculture in much the same terms that conservatives criticized his policies. He was appalled by the "regimentation" involved in the cost of production plan, and he termed the Bankhead bill's provisions for compulsory cotton control "abhorrent."[32] Franklin Roosevelt at a 1936 press conference discussed the possibility of an export subsidy program for agriculture. Asked whether it would "be possible . . . to subsidize the export of a limited amount of each crop so as to avoid the inducement to plow up additional land," FDR responded, "If I were a dictator, it probably could be worked. That is the best answer to that."[33]

Those concerned with the problem of crop control enforcement often drew an analogy with prohibition. Conservative GOP Senator Robert Carey, for example, warned that if the AAA "bill becomes . . . law, we will have a new bootlegger—the bootlegger of agricultural products."[34] David Reed characterized the Bankhead bill as "a new kind of prohibition law," adding that "it will take the whole American Army to enforce its provisions."[35] Simeon Fess asked, "If we could not enforce prohibition, how can we enforce this [Bankhead] . . . plan . . . ?"[36] Again, not only conservatives, but also New Dealers and radicals, advanced this analogy. Norman Thomas argued that the Bankhead bill would "have all the difficulties that attended the enforcement of prohibition," that it would require "an army of snoopers."[37]

Secretary Wallace recorded that five farm state governors in the fall of 1933 urged the President "to put into effect compulsory marketing control for every farm product. . . . I shuddered. I thought of the racketeering that would grow up at once. . . . I thought of Prohibition. . . ."[38]

Crop control was not the New Deal's only response to the farm problem—it also sought to expand domestic and foreign markets for farm products—but restriction was its immediate reaction to the 1933 crisis, and part of its overall effort to restore economic equilibrium through planning. Under crop restriction, the argument went, farm prices would rise, agriculture would regain parity with industry, and general recovery would be spurred. A product of the chaos of the early thirties, crop control legislation was again pushed during the surplus crisis of 1937. Yet crop control, like spending, was a program about which even its supporters could be ambivalent; like spending it was presented as an "emergency" and "artificial" device to be utilized pending the restoration of "normal" conditions.

Foes of crop control appeared from across the ideological spectrum; the New Deal's limited "middle way" in agriculture could be and was buffeted from all sides. Opposition to crop control was part and parcel of the general opposition to "scarcity economics" which all varieties of critics—progressive, conservative, and radical alike—charged characterized the New Deal. The AAA—like the NRA—could be opposed by progressives, conservatives, and farm state men of varied sorts, by purchasing power thesis men, antimonopoly men, classical economy-confidence thesis men, exports expansion men, money men, and others on grounds that were ideologically consistent with their overall positions and philosophies. This made schemes like the AAA and NRA vulnerable, especially insofar as they were presented by their proponents as emergency measures to begin with; they could be opposed at least as permanent formulae by members of virtually all political and ideological groups.

Opposition to crop control on the ground that its "sales" tax curtailed consumption, like the opposition to its scarcity economics, came from varied sources; it provided an example of

how individuals of otherwise diverse persuasions—Norman
Thomas, Jerry Voorhis, Carter Glass, Hamilton Fish, William
Borah—could unite; it illustrated the ideological vulnerability of
the New Deal's limited "middle way." Its "sales" tax could be
denounced on classical economy grounds (government should
not obstruct the free working of the economic processes); on the
grounds of economic equilibrium—and urban interest (the higher
prices wrought by crop control were injurious to industrial workers and consumers); and on the related grounds of the purchasing
power thesis (buying power should be increased rather than production curtailed). While proponents argued that crop control
was expressly designed to implement that thesis by expanding
farmers' incomes, critics such as Borah answered that the crucial
need was to expand the purchasing power of farmers and non-
farmers together, not to take from one to give to the other.

Many held that the NRA, by raising the prices of the products the farmer had to buy, was undoing the AAA attempt to
restore parity for agriculture. This argument was advanced by
conservatives, but it was also expressed by Norman Thomas, and
by a wide array of farm state men. This was the other side of
the AAA's "sales" tax coin, with agriculture's spokesmen now
reversing roles with urban political leaders. The NRA-AAA controversy, in turn, was related to the overall concept of economic
balance. Just as defenders of the AAA argued that the higher
prices to consumers wrought by crop control were outweighed
by the increased demand for industrial products provided by a
prosperous agricultural community, defenders of NRA in a farm
context argued that any adverse agricultural impact NRA may
have had was more than offset by the increased market for farm
products provided by more prosperous workers. Each advanced
a concept of economic interdependence, each argued that farmers
and workers were indeed interdependent, but each parted from
the other over the practical programs through which the concept
was to be instituted.

The NRA-AAA debate drove in some ways to the core of
the New Deal approach. As GOP Congressman Everett Dirksen
stated the dilemma, the AAA raised the prices of farm products
sold to consumers, and the NRA raised the prices of products

the farmer had to buy, "and once again we get into the vicious circle of seeking a balance and not knowing precisely where to begin."[39] The objective was balance, but where to begin? How could the efforts to achieve balance in the various sectors be so coordinated as to bring balance to the economy as a whole— especially if there was (as under the New Deal schema) no central plan expressly designed to coordinate the various sector plans and programs to this end? Within the general context of crop control this query could be raised by men of varied ideological persuasions: by radicals, who considered a central, coordinating plan essential; by conservatives, who argued that planning would upset the economy's equilibrium; and by farm state men of varying persuasions, whose key concern remained parity for agriculture.

The crux of the matter once again dealt with the nature of the New Deal effort to implement the purchasing power thesis, with the New Deal's limited planning programs, and with their implications for the planning philosophy per se. For under the AAA, the planning philosophy was identified with production restriction, rather than with potential abundance. This was a result of the New Deal's unwillingness to go too far beyond the bounds of traditional orthodoxy, to engage, for example, in a type of planning which would give some coordinated direction to such individual agencies as the AAA and the NRA. The New Dealers recognized the potential for abundance in America's capacity to produce, but—given their commitment to the capitalist "system" per se—they failed to transcend the barriers which (in their own terms) stood in the way of the creation of the consumptive capacity necessary to release that potential productive abundance.

Critics further alleged that crop control (and economic planning per se, as conservatives saw it) fueled commodity conflicts within agriculture; they held that it could lead to scrambles for special privilege; and the conservatives among them contended that it could end—given the self-generating characteristics of economic planning—by turning agriculture into a completely controlled sector. This in turn was related to the largely (but not wholly) conservative criticism that crop control was autocratic, and that it was analogous to prohibition in the problems of enforcement that it posed. In its major, and conservative, version this criticism was part of the overall right-wing opposition to New Deal "regimentation," to planned economy, to deviations from the economic institutions of nineteenth-century liberalism. Essentially a conservative criticism, it was also employed by William Borah and Norman Thomas in their cases against crop control, and it was employed by New Dealers Wallace and Roosevelt in their arguments against proposed alternatives.

ALTERNATIVES

Out of the potpourri of farm programs put forth in 1933, the Roosevelt administration chose crop control. Critics of the choice —conservatives, progressives, radicals, and assorted Democrats alike—all stressed the need to devise a program that would avoid the alleged deficiencies of production restriction. During the first trying months of the AAA, especially, calls for currency expansion were pronounced; other proposed routes to farm recovery included varieties of McNary-Haugenism, as well as increased industrial-urban purchasing power (so as to expand the market for farm products). Many of crop control's reluctant supporters, of course, looked to a restoration of "normal" trade relations as a permanent solution. These various alternatives were advanced by men who considered the AAA inadequate, and by men who considered the AAA abhorrent, by rural and urban representatives; withal by men of otherwise varying political and ideological persuasions.

One group in 1933 called for monetary remedies. Latter-day populists, they hailed largely from farm states, the South, West, and Midwest. Currency expansion, they argued, would lighten the farmer's debt load and give him greater equality vis-à-vis industry. During the AAA debate, and as farm prices declined in the fall of 1933, the cry for inflation was strong. Monetary sentiment ebbed as AAA benefits began to flow,[40] but the strain persisted. North Carolina Senator Robert Reynolds, for example, stressing the need for currency expansion, declared in 1934 that with it "such legislation as this [Bankhead cotton control bill] would not be necessary."[41] Cotton Ed Smith complained in 1935 that instead of expanding the currency, "we are approaching the subject from the other end, and . . . are going to reduce production . . . to the scarcity of money."[42]

Varieties of McNary-Haugenism were advanced by conservative Republicans as alternatives to both crop control and reciprocal trade; by some southern Democrats, concerned with expediting cotton exports; and by various farm state men. Those who favored such proposals often stressed that they would not involve the "regimentation," "bureaucracy," and other flaws of crop control. Vermont Governor George Aiken, for example, having endorsed one such plan, noted that "all this can be done without detriment to the . . . purchasing power of the industrial worker, without imposing production control on the farmer, and without destroying the foreign market for his surplus."[43] Senator Charles McNary similarly contended in 1938 that "the farmer can be helped in ways that will neither give away his markets by tariff concessions and crop restriction nor set up regiments of inspectors to police him into compliance with marketing quotas. Long before the present Administration . . . I favored bills to give the farmer . . . aid by means of an equalization fee or export debentures, and I believe that something of that nature could yet be made effective."[44]

Texas Democrat Tom Connally proposed an export debenture plan designed to spur agricultural, and especially cotton, exports, stimulate farm recovery, provide farmers with a tariff equivalent, and restore economic equilibrium between agriculture and industry. (But this approach, while rationalized as a way to avoid internal controls, and attractive to those who sought an "easy" and external remedy, also, like crop control, had further implications and complications of its own. In defense of his debenture plan, for example, Connally declared: "That is the only way . . . you are going to raise the domestic price to the producer, increase the cost to the consumer." The consumer paid crop control's processing tax; the consumer would pay for the debenture plan, too, "just as he has been paying it [through the protective tariff] for a hundred years in the case of . . . manu-factured articles. . . .")[45]

Many leaders pointed to the economic interdependence of agriculture and industry, arguing that increased industrial employment would expand the market for farm products, that increased buying power among workers could best ensure the revival and maintenance of agricultural prosperity. This theme was pursued by conservative Republicans such as Knox, Hoover, and Mills, who, given the probusiness orientation of their confidence thesis, would be expected to consider the restoration of industrial prosperity basic, and by such New Dealers as Roosevelt and Wallace.[46] Robert Wagner, for example, proceeding (like other men of the left) from the purchasing power thesis, conceded that crop reduction might be essential as a temporary expedient, but contended that it would be ruinous as a permanent policy. "There will be no permanent or satisfying solution [to the farm problem]," he held, "until we bring about a condition where the . . . wage-earning population . . . will get a fair share of the wealth. . . ."[47]

William Borah declared in 1936 that "under a sound economic system" the domestic market would be "ample to insure . . . return of prosperity to agriculture." "It is here in the United States . . . that our markets must be found. And they can never be found until we restore purchasing power. . . . You can never restore purchasing power while private interests . . . fix prices. The farm . . . problem, therefore, has its roots in the most profound problem in our whole social structure." As Borah saw it, the crux of the farm problem (as of the entire economic problem) was monopoly price-fixing. Whatever might be done to increase the farmer's income, monopolies could undo by hiking their prices on what he had to buy. Monopoly prices kept the people from developing sufficient purchasing power to provide what would otherwise be an ample domestic market for farm products. If the people could buy what they needed there would be no overproduction on American farms.[48]

Alternatives to crop control were advanced from across the ideological spectrum; even crop control's proponents, after all,

looked elsewhere for more permanent cures, seeing in production restriction (like pump priming) an emergency and artificial
expedient. The call for the currency expansion alternative was a
popular one, especially in 1933. It was presented as an "easy"
remedy; adopt it, the argument ran, and resort to the scarcity
economics of crop control, to coercion, to bureaucracy, need not
be had. Currency expansion and production restriction would both
raise farm prices, but the one would do it without the ruin and
regimentation inherent in the other.

Others dissatisfied with crop control revived McNary-
Haugenism; plans of this vintage, proponents argued, would restore agriculture, retain foreign markets, and do it without coercive regimentation. Such schemes had a widespread appeal.
They could appeal to protectionist Republicans who could see in
them not only a farm program but also an alternative to the
hated experiment in reciprocity; to at least some southern Democrats intent upon spurring the cotton export trade; to those looking for an agricultural equivalent to industry's tariff; to those
who were concerned that crop control was losing foreign markets for American farm exports (and to those who considered a
large volume of exports essential to the domestic prosperity of
American agriculture); to those who disliked the concept of
scarcity per se; to those who disliked crop control's high prices
for urban consumers; and to all those who disliked crop control's
"bureaucracy," "regimentation," and "autocracy."

Others emphasized the home market, arguing that the expanded outlet for farm products provided by a prosperous working
class constituted a key to agricultural recovery. This view was
advanced by New Dealers as well as by conservative Republicans,
clearly dovetailing with the purchasing power thesis of the former
and the confidence thesis-business recovery orientation of the
latter. Some further related this theme to monopoly, arguing
that it constituted the obstruction to farm—and to general—
recovery. William Borah, for example, rejecting the "easy" argument that because industrialists curtailed production farmers
were justified in doing the same, contended that action should
be directed at the cause of the malady (monopoly) rather than
at its symptom (the farm problem). Here Borah went beyond

those who focused on the farm problem per se, and who often supported various farm remedies with their eyes focused narrowly upon the agricultural sector rather than on the remedies' implications for the economy as a whole. Borah's whole point, on the other hand, was that the farm problem could not be solved by a farm program, that the farm problem was part of the economic problem as a whole and could only be solved by a general remedy, that Americans should confront the real problem (in Borah's terms, monopoly) rather than opting for emergency expedients, halfway remedies, contrived devices, and so on, all designed to relieve problems rather than truly to resolve them.

5

ECONOMIC PLANNING

The New Dealers did not embrace systematic planning even in 1933–34; their concept tended to be vague and limited. The conservatives' critique of planning, based squarely upon their confidence thesis and classical economy assumptions, was sharply dogmatic. The NRA, a chief planning agency, was designed by the New Dealers to help implement the purchasing power thesis. But their eventual ambivalence over NRA again evidenced the gap between the purchasing power thesis per se and the problems inherent in the New Dealers' unwillingness to transcend traditional ideology in order to implement it. The New Dealers' own dogmatism, their lack of coordinated planning, their inability to cope with private economic power, all frustrated their efforts to use NRA to balance the economy and to implement the thesis. The NRA, moreover, given its limited "middle way" character, was sharply attacked by both left and right: by the right in terms of the conservative critique of the planning philosophy, by the left for its failure to implement the purchasing power thesis. With the NRA's demise, alternatives were looked to which would avoid its deficiencies, and (in the case of the left) more effectively implement the purchasing power thesis. These alternatives further evidenced the decline of planning and the growing strength of antimonopolism by the later thirties.

PLANNING

"Planning" was in intellectual vogue during the thirties, especially circa 1933, less so as the epochal mood of that year declined; it was a key concept of the depression years, advanced by many as an alternative to the old era of laissez-faire and "rugged individualism." It was a concept rooted in the intellectual currents of the late nineteenth century and of the progressive era, in the writings of such men as Simon Patten, Thorstein Veblen, and Herbert Croly. It was advanced during the thirties in schemes of many varieties offered by economists, and by business, labor, farm, and citizens' groups. Franklin Roosevelt sometimes spoke of "planning" during the 1932 campaign, and his entourage included several planners of various sorts, among them Rexford G. Tugwell, Columbia University economist. Thus planning in 1933 had a distinguished intellectual heritage, a depression context in which the concept of laissez-faire had become discredited, and an administration in power which looked favorably upon it at least in general terms.

Yet, as with the cleavage between an Eccles and the politicos over spending, so, too, was there a cleavage between a Tugwell and the politicos over planning. Radicals, to be sure, did embrace the planning philosophy; conservatives, to be sure, tended not to distinguish between the various types of planning, linking them all to the planned economies of autocratic states, and denouncing them accordingly; still, there were several varieties of planning, ranging from those designed to replace capitalism to those designed to revive and readjust the existing economic order, of which the New Deal's was a distinctly limited version. The concept was related by its proponents to the mature economy theme (planning was now essential to economic stability), to the production-consumption disequilibrium (planning would help implement the purchasing power thesis), and to the disparity between agriculture and industry (planning would help correct the disparity).

The New Deal's efforts at planning were most clearly illustrated by the AAA and the NRA, but New Dealers also spoke in more general terms. Robert Wagner, for example declared in

1933 that "a new economic society has come to its full maturity," an industrial order which had to function as an integrated and balanced whole if it was to function successfully at all.[1] Henry Wallace argued that with the decline of the free market mechanism planning was essential to restore economic equilibrium.[2] Franklin Roosevelt, espousing a mild and flexible version of the planning philosophy, called for the establishment of economic equilibrium. "What we are trying to do," he explained in 1936, "is to bring about a balanced system of economy in the United States. . . ."[3]

Others conceded that extraordinary measures had to be taken to restore the economy, but contended that such measures were purely emergency phenomena, to be discarded as the emergency passed; this was part and parcel of the general emergency rationale of the era, the theme (so often sounded in the spending context, for example) that a return to orthodoxy was in order once the crisis was over. It was a stance taken especially by men whose positions lay between those who looked to planning as at least a vaguely permanent phenomenon and those who adhered to the natural recovery propositions of classical economics. Jimmy Byrnes provided an example. When the NRA and AAA "have brought about an adjustment of production to consumption," the South Carolinian asserted, ". . . government [must] cease its regulation of business. . . ." "When the emergency passes, they must pass. For permanent prosperity . . . we must rely upon private enterprise. . . ."[4]

Others rejected the concept of planning virtually in toto. Free the economy from governmental restraints, they argued, allow "economic laws" to operate, and recovery would appear automatically. New Deal attempts to order the economy were "artificial" and doomed to fail; they were the very preventives of "natural" recovery. Among those pursuing this theme, a corollary in the planning context of the conservatives' overall classical economy-confidence thesis-natural recovery assumptions, were Republicans Knox, Dickinson, and David Reed, and Democrats Glass, Bailey, and John W. Davis.[5] As Davis saw it, "most of the economic illnesses of the . . . world are directly traceable to government. . . ."[6] Legislation, Senators Byrd, Copeland, and

Frederick Hale all agreed, would never restore prosperity.[7] "Recovery from this depression is inevitable," Herbert Hoover concluded, "though it may be slowed up by government policies."[8]

Some argued that the New Deal contemplated not only "artificial" devices to spur recovery, but an "artificial" structure to replace the existing economy, that it was bent upon replacing what was both the "American" and the "natural" system (a neat convergence in the conservative mind). William H. King, for example, charged that "There are those within executive departments who believe in artificial policies and who are trying to build an artificial economic . . . system. . . ."[9] L. J. Dickinson asserted that "The proposition now advanced is to supersede the workings of economic law through the establishment of a vast federal bureaucracy . . . in supreme control of the nation's economic life. The belief is held out that a synthetic . . . prosperity can be induced . . . by reconstructing all economic relationships. . . ." This artificial system, he contended, created new disparities and new disequilibriums without eradicating existing ones; it created an economy "more and more . . . dependent upon . . . artificial restoratives."[10]

Conservatives further contended that the economy was too big and too complex to be directed from one central point. As Ogden Mills put it, "there exists . . . no man or group of men who can visualize, much less direct, the [complexities] . . . of American economic life."[11] As evidence conservatives pointed to the internal contradictions of New Deal planning. One planning policy, they argued, tended to cancel out another: while AAA raised the farmer's prices, for example, NRA raised the prices of the products he had to buy; NRA might have helped workers, but AAA raised their food prices; reciprocal trade conflicted with domestic programs—and so on.[12] (Socialist Norman Thomas, on the hand, agreed that New Deal policies contradicted one another, but argued that the contradictions were inherent in the capitalist system, of which the New Deal was only an expression.)[13]

Another major conservative criticism of planning was that it could not remain partial, that the more planning intruded into the economy the more it created maladjustments in the normally self-adjusting processes of capitalism and the more it required still further intrusion, that any attempts at partial planning would automatically generate pervasive planning, and that "economic planning" would necessarily end in "planned economy." Lewis Douglas, for example, argued that "the confusion created by the effect of plans in one field of . . . endeavor running counter to . . . plans in another—the extent to which a plan in one segment of enterprise nullifies a plan for another segment—gives rise to a demand for further and further plans. And so the plans lead on to other plans. . . ."[14]

Critics of planning also alleged that it would stifle progress, creating a static economic order. A planned economy, they contended, could perhaps bring stability, but lacking the dynamism of free enterprise it could not bring expansion. It would deaden those creative energies of free men and free enterprisers that were the very spirit and substance of economic progress. Free enterprise, they argued, was *the* system of abundance; all other systems were scarcity systems; planned economy was just such a scarcity system; NRA and AAA provided contemporary examples. Hoover, Mills, Douglas, and Knox all pursued this theme.[15] It was, like the conservatives' criticisms of planning generally, a theme which clearly flowed from and cohered with their overall classical economy-confidence thesis natural recovery assumptions—their overall view of what a successful economy was and how it worked.

Criticism of New Deal planning came from the radical left as well as from the conservative right. Tom Amlie, for example, argued that the New Deal's philosophy was to prop up the profit system through the institutionalization of scarcity economics. The New Deal, he asserted, was trying to coordinate an economy without any means of coordinating the coordinators; it was trying futilely to plan "without a central plan."[16] Norman Thomas also frequently criticized attempts at planning within a New Deal or essentially capitalist framework. He declared in 1933 that the "N.R.A. has not even sought to provide a general economic plan." To be successful "even on its own terms . . . over any considerable length of time the New Deal must give us rapidly . . . general economic planning as against the attempt to consider agriculture and each industry as a separate unit. . . ." New Deal "planning," he added, often consisted of nothing more than subsidies to privileged economic groups.[17]

Robert Jackson, a leading public spokesman for the New Deal by 1937–38, was a strong critic of certain concepts of economic planning. He argued that industrial self-regulation sanctified the status quo; he contended that the public interest could not be represented in planning short of actual political participation in the management of industry; he held that planning, to be successful, had to be pervasive. Like the conservatives, he insisted that planned stability would end in economic stagnation. (Yet Jackson—here parting with the conservatives—also asserted on occasion that measures such as the AAA, the Guffey coal bill, minimum wage laws, and the like could provide the economy with a needed degree of stability and equilibrium, permitting the "competitive system . . . [to] work without the social costs which competition . . . involved in the past.")[18]

Not only a Robert Jackson, of course, but also New Dealers with a clear commitment to a variety of planning were very circumspect as to how far planning should be allowed to proceed; like the conservatives, they, too, saw danger points; like the conservatives, they argued that planning—once it got beyond those points—threatened all sorts of horror. Henry Wallace, for example, urged that planning deal only with "broad outlines"; direct, detailed planning by government he considered an open door to "regimentation."[19] Robert Wagner declared in 1938 that "as a general proposition" he "opposed . . . legislation fixing anything except a minimum wage. . . . If we ever . . . pass laws . . . to fix all . . . wages, we will destroy . . . freedom of collective bargaining and advance on the road toward fascism."[20] Queried about Wagner's statement, no less a New Dealer than Franklin Roosevelt declared, "It goes in line with everything I have always said. . . ."[21]

There was not very much positive, well-articulated, and systematic support for the planning philosophy among New Dealers. Their approach to planning (as to spending) was a limited and hesitant one; their particular programs—the NRA and the AAA —reflected this ideological ambivalence; they were reluctant planners as well as reluctant spenders both in theory and practice. Others were even more reluctant than they; middling Democrats, for example, caught between the rigid conservative foes of planning and the limited planners of the New Deal persuasion, caught also perhaps between party loyalty and philosophical tendency, approved of planning solely on an emergency basis, or went along even with the administration's mild experiments reluctantly.

Critics of planning, imbued with the verities of classical economics, and insistent that the economy could restore itself, saw in planning the very dire qualities that planners saw in the existing economy. Where planners associated chaos and depression with unregulated capitalism, conservatives regarded free enterprise as inherently self-adjusting and dynamic. Where planners thought that a coordinated economy would usher in recovery, conservatives argued that its consequences would be maladjustment and institutionalized depression. Specifically, the conservatives argued that planning was "artificial" and obstructed the workings of natural economic law, that the economy was too big and too complex to plan, that the various planning programs contradicted one another, that planning so upset the economy's equilibrium that the planners would in the end be forced to control and regiment the entire system, that a planned order lacked the dynamism of a free economy and would necessarily be frozen and static.

As the conservatives' rejection of planning flowed from their confidence and natural recovery assumptions and was part of their overall view of how the economy worked (planning would disrupt the system's equilibrium, destroy confidence, delay recovery), the radicals' case against *New Deal* planning flowed from their overall view of the economic order. The radicals' essential point was that the New Deal lacked a central, coordinating plan; underlying this was the assumption that capitalism could not be saved, and that efforts to implement the purchasing power thesis through planning would not work within the capitalist frame. But while the underlying assumptions on which radicals and conservatives based their critiques were opposed, their specific criticisms sometimes converged. They agreed, for example, that the New Deal's limited planning could not of itself succeed, and that its logical sequence was central planning—advocated by radicals and abhorrent to conservatives. Both groups of critics agreed that New Deal plans were contradictory, though they differed on the nature of the contradictions, the conservatives seeing them inherent in the New Deal's divergence from capitalism, the radicals seeing them inherent in the very capitalism which the New Deal was vainly attempting to reform. The New Dealers, on the other hand, joined with the conservatives in denouncing the radicals' demand for general, centralized planning; they tinkered more than they planned; they once again took their dogmatically limited "middle way" with all its practical implications and consequences.

NRA

The National Recovery Administration had varied roots. It was a depression remedy, but it went back to the New Nationalist progressive tradition, and more specifically to the World War I War Industries Board; it was part of the general vogue for planning of the early thirties, but it also reflected the 1920s penchant for trade associations; it partook of the plans for recovery offered by various business groups with schemes for "cooperation" and "coordination" to end the chaos of "cutthroat" competition, and it was looked to by those of a social reformist bent to end child labor and "sweatshop" conditions, to reduce workers' hours and to raise their wages. The National Industrial Recovery Act was passed in 1933 with opposition from both conservatives and antimonopoly progressives; its popularity among both the public and the politicos waned as its performance in the view of many lagged far behind its promise; it was finally declared unconstitutional by the Supreme Court in 1935.

The National Recovery Administration, together with the AAA, constituted the New Deal's central approach to the concept of planning. On signing the NIRA in June 1933 Franklin Roosevelt declared that "It represents a supreme effort to stabilize ... the many factors which make for the prosperity of the Nation, and the preservation of American standards."[22] The President's statement illustrated the variety of planning the NRA was to involve; it implied a distinctly limited version; the call was for a "stabilized" rather than a "planned" economy. The phrase "preservation of American standards" implied the key to stabilization; the NRA was widely seen as a means to eradicate such "unfair" practices as long hours, low wages, and monopoly price-slashing, to prevent "cutthroat" competition, to implement the purchasing power thesis. Thus the New Deal's limited planning concept, the "cutthroat" competition rationale, and the purchasing power thesis were all intertwined in the case for the NRA.

Various proponents advanced this multifaceted theme. George Earle, for example, who thought the NIRA "the greatest law ever written," argued that "In its net effect it was anything but monopolistic." The NIRA's "fundamental principle" was the establishment of higher wages and shorter hours.[23] Frank Murphy argued in early 1937 that the wages and hours provisions of the NRA were its "most important and soundest features . . . and on that solid basis of . . . widely distributed purchasing power, our present recovery was based."[24] Congressman John McCormack contended in 1936 that "The N.R.A., as originally passed, was never intended as permanent legislation," but that something was "going to come out of" it. "Industry cannot continue subject to the unfair competition of the unscrupulous 10 percent. . . . Ninety percent of business men . . . want to pay their employees a living wage; want to give them reasonable working hours; but cannot because of the unscrupulous competition of a small minority."[25]

Ellis Hawley writes that much of the 1933 congressional debate over the NIRA "centered about the efforts of Administration spokesmen to convince . . . old-line progressives . . . that the measure would strengthen the competitive system rather than destroy it."[26] Spokesmen for a proposal that moved—even so slightly as did the NRA—toward the planning philosophy still found it necessary to speak in terms of "competition," to proceed with all due respect for traditional concepts, to pay homage to the ancient verities—even in so seemingly epochal and "revolutionary" a year as 1933. Robert Wagner, the Senate's leading proponent of the measure, was among those sounding this theme. "If this legislation passes," he declared in June 1933, "it will be the first time that small business will have a voice in the government of industry." He was "in fundamental agreement with the objectives of the Senator from Idaho [Borah]." He agreed "that what we must provide against above all else are monopolies and monopolistic practices."[27]

Wagner's rationale during the early period, in pushing the NRA, was that while the antitrust laws were designed to prevent the excessive concentration of wealth and to protect small businessmen, workers, and consumers, this method had slight chance of success from the beginning; it was based on Adam Smith's *Wealth of Nations;* it could not meet the conditions of modern industrialism. The antitrust laws had failed to check the growth in the size of business or the concentration of private economic power; large-scale enterprise was the inevitable result of technological change; it could not be arrested by law. But the antitrust laws did force business to grow big by methods that were injurious to small businessmen, workers, and consumers. Since the law forbade the association of independent business groups, business expanded through ruthless and predatory methods; businessmen vied with one another by cutting wages and lengthening hours of work. Small businessmen were not allowed to meet the challenge of big business by cooperating with one another. They, too, were forced into a destructive, cutthroat competition. And with cutthroat competition big businesses had been able to destroy small ones.[28]

Wagner insisted that the NIRA was designed not to abolish competition but to place it on a higher plane by striking at unfair practices. Most businesses wished to pay higher wages and to shorten hours, but without some sort of national system they could be undercut by the ruthless few. NRA was designed to promote reemployment by promoting order in industry, to spur recovery by removing the barriers to it, to introduce economic planning on a national scale. All business today was affected with a public interest; therefore it was within the realm of government to act. NRA retained voluntarism and competition. It sought to fulfill the objectives of the antitrust legislation. Under present conditions a few could drag all business down by paying low wages and lengthening working hours and thereby forcing reluctant competitors to do the same in order to stay in business. NRA was designed to protect small businessmen against such predatory practices.[29]

As the NRA progressed, however, Wagner's initial enthusiasm gave way to a more critical attitude. He denounced business control of the codes, urged that industry, labor, and government act in concert, and warned that intrabusiness cooperation alone would end in diminished purchasing power and intensified disequilibrium. Wagner granted in 1935, "I am in sympathy with the Senator [Borah] as to price fixing. I had never supposed when we passed the act that the . . . 'price-fixing power' would be exercised as it had been." "I have held, from the very inception of the . . . Act, that price fixing, when it goes beyond the bounds of establishing minimum wages and prohibiting the cut-throat practice of selling below cost, has no place in a program designed to shield the individual business man against . . . monopoly." In 1937 Wagner added that "we . . . tried the NIRA, presuming that cooperation was more productive than strife. But . . . there were important oversights. It was forgotten that while big business was fully prepared to 'cooperate' in its own behalf, neither the government nor the public had developed the vigilant techniques required to keep this new freedom within appropriate bounds. . . ."[30]

Yet on balance and in retrospect Wagner's overall evaluation of NRA was not unfavorable, and here he reflected the characteristic New Deal ambivalence toward the agency. He argued that in place of "destructive planlessness" NRA had expedited reemployment, shorter hours, and stable wages. He declared in 1936 that "one of the reasons why there has not been the increase [in employment] that there should have been . . . is because the National Recovery Act was held unconstitutional." Under NRA "unemployment . . . was gradually being absorbed as a result of the code provisions. . . . Hours were being decreased rapidly. . . ." Since NRA "was declared unconstitutional hours have increased, and . . . wages have not increased. . . . By the extension of hours the productive capacity per worker has been increased, and he has not been given the . . . purchasing power to absorb the . . .

products . . . we are producing." That was "why there has been
a retardment of unemployment absorption."[31]

Franklin Roosevelt did not look to the NRA fundamentally
to restructure the economy, but rather urged support for it in
1933 as a means through which business, labor, and government
could cooperate to eradicate "unfair" competition, improve
wages, shorten hours, and increase employment. Stressing that
the antitrust laws remained firm against monopolistic price-fixing, he asserted that the objective was "to restore our rich domestic market by raising its vast consuming capacity. If we now
inflate prices as fast and as far as we increase wages, the whole
project will be set at naught. . . . In these first critical months . . .
we [must] defer price increases as long as possible." The President also spoke in broader terms: ". . . we seek . . . balance in our
economic system. . . ." NRA's "very conception . . . follows the
democratic procedure of our Government. . . . Its theory of self-
regulation follows the American method rather than any of the
experiments being tried in other Nations."[32]

By the end of 1933 Roosevelt, like Wagner, was expressing
concern about NRA's direction. He worried that "the operation
of some of the codes may work out in such a way that big business
will be benefited to the detriment of . . . little businesses. . . . Certain developments would tend to show that some industries believe that the Sherman Anti-Trust Law principle has, in some
mysterious way, been abolished by the NRA Act which, of
course, is not so." He also had retrospective criticisms. Writing
in 1937, he observed that the codes were controlled by "organized producers and sellers," and were administered in their interests rather than those of consumers. "It had become evident by
[March 1934] . . . that the N.R.A. lacked any general agreement,
either among leaders in industry or . . . Government, upon . . .
fundamental economic policies. . . ."[33]

Yet Roosevelt, again like Wagner, continued to insist on the
essential validity of NRA's underlying principles. In 1936 he suggested "that the National Recovery Act . . . accomplished as much
for the restoration of prosperity, through the . . . minimum wage,
the shortening of hours and . . . elimination of child labor, as any
law . . . of the Federal Government in the past century and a

half." He argued in 1937 that NRA helped "small . . . business men . . . by the establishment of fair competition and the elimination of such monopolistic practices as destructive price cutting." And looking back on the NRA from the perspective of the recession in late 1937, FDR discussed the advance of recovery by mid-decade: "The time was just after the NRA decision. Wages and hours were all right. . . . There was . . . the getting together of industry . . . around a table . . . where they went over the . . . law of supply and demand," reviewing the needs of the economy. "That was knocked into a cocked hat."[34]

Others similarly expressed shifting or uneasy support for the NRA. Maury Maverick, for example, declared in 1935 that "the N.R.A. must be continued—that is, we must have regulation of industry and protection for the rights of labor and of . . . consumers. . . ." He conceded that the NRA restricted production, that the codes were American equivalents of the "European price cartel," that combines fixed prices while labor's rights went unprotected, that perhaps "we Democrats are adopting the Republican doctrine of big business," that NRA was "poorly administered" and "something of a failure," but he insisted that it should have been improved upon rather than discarded. Maverick in 1937 added that "if the N.R.A. had been worked backward, that is, pay high wages and have unlimited production," there might have been more purchasing power, more production, more consumption, and adequate profits.[35]

Others were skeptical about NRA from the very beginning. Conservatives, of course, attacked it for its "regimentation" of industry, and as a disruptive deviation from the processes of the American system, an illustration of the failings of the planning philosophy.[36] From the left it was attacked for its big business price-fixing, and for its failure—despite its rationale—to implement the purchasing power thesis. As Bronson Cutting put it, "The one chance . . . for the N.R.A. to have been successful was the building up of the purchasing power of the country; and that meant . . . that wages would have to rise more rapidly than prices. . . . The reverse has been the case. . . ."[37] Norman Thomas agreed that under NRA big business price-fixing was condoned, profits outran wages, and the problem of income maldistribution remained unresolved.[38]

Hugo Black charged in 1933 that the NIRA did not meet the central need for a more equitable distribution of the national income, that it was not geared to implementation of the purchasing power thesis. A larger share should go to workers, he argued, and a smaller share to capital; wages should be high, prices low; yet the NIRA involved "an abandonment of the competitive system . . . in large part." It took from consumers the benefit of low prices resulting from competitive processes, but offered no method to control unduly high prices. If the competitive system was to be abandoned as to price regulation, the Alabaman insisted, then it was essential that the government itself regulate prices. If the purchasing power thesis was to be implemented under the NIRA, then profits would have to be regulated and restricted. He accordingly "would have added to the part of the bill giving the right to fix . . . minimum wages the words 'maximum profits.' "[39]

Antimonopoly progressives William Borah and Gerald Nye joined in this criticism. The need was for a more equitable distribution of income, Borah asserted, but NRA had a contrary impact, expanding big business profits. The need was for high wages and low prices, but under NRA monopoly prices nullified wage increases, reduced purchasing power, and retarded recovery. Small business was driven from the field, and big business commanded the codes.[40] Nye charged that under NRA the power of monopoly had increased, big business price-fixing was permitted, prices to consumers were being fixed at inordinately high levels, and competition was being stifled. Profits of capital were increased far beyond any gains won by labor; the real need was for greatly increased mass buying power, and NRA's was a contrary effect.[41]

The NRA's interrelated rationale—calling for an end to "cutthroat" competition, for limited planning (shading over into industrial self-regulation), for implementation of the purchasing power thesis through higher wages and shorter hours—raised a plethora of questions about its own internal consistency, about the efficacy of the New Deal's limited planning, and about whether the purchasing power thesis could be instituted in an essentially capitalist frame. If slashed prices could be based upon low wages and long hours, for example, could they not also be a boon to consumers? If a boon to consumers, though, how could consumptive capacity be expanded if workers received inadequate wages? If higher prices would permit higher wages and shorter hours, would they not still be injurious to consumers? If injurious to consumers, were they not however a boon to workers? How— given the limited planning and voluntarism of the NRA approach —could wage hikes be kept ahead of those of prices? How could it be guaranteed that higher prices would be passed on to workers in higher wages? How could business be kept from raising prices unduly?

The NRA was further part and parcel of the New Deal's dogmatically limited "middle way," advancing toward planning but justified in the name of "fair" competition, calling for institution of the purchasing power thesis but relying upon voluntarism. Like the cases for public spending and crop control, its rationale reflected the unwillingness or inability of political leaders to break loose from the bonds of traditional American ideology. As with public spending and crop control, New Dealers as an ideological type were fundamentally ambivalent about the NRA. Proponents of the purchasing power thesis, "balance," and "planning," they were chagrined by prices which outran wages, by business control of the codes, by "planning" that retarded recovery. Foes of unfair competitive practices, such as monopoly price cutting, they feared that NRA was fostering monopoly price-fixing. Yet, despite their doubts and disappointments, men such as Roosevelt and Wagner argued that NRA accomplished much, particularly in the area of wages and hours, that it had, albeit imperfectly, moved toward implementation of the purchasing power thesis, and that its invalidation therefore impeded the advance of recovery and reform.

The ambiguity and ambivalence of New Dealers over NRA's results were reflective of the overall New Deal approach. As with the relationship (or lack of one) between the AAA and the NRA, the case of the latter per se illustrated the difficulties inherent in the New Deal's limited approach. The New Dealers' attempt to institute the purchasing power thesis was stymied (in their own terms) by the power of big business, yet their ideological inhibitions prevented them from confronting that power through alternative programs (such as central planning and public ownership). Like the AAA, the NRA associated the planning philosophy with restrictive practices, and thereby discredited it in the eyes of many—an especially ironic fact in that NRA, under business hegemony, constituted an agency quite unlike that envisaged by genuine planners.

Critics of NRA formed a variegated coalition; the New Deal's limited "middle way" in industry was a target for attack from all sides. Adversaries ranged from those on the radical left, who denounced it as an institutionalization of the scarcity economics of capitalism, to those on the conservative right, who denounced it as an institutionalization of the scarcity economics of New Dealism. It was opposed by antimonopoly progressives, who saw in it a sanctification of trusts, and by conservatives, who insisted that it destroyed free market processes. It was attacked by proponents of the purchasing power thesis (who argued that it accentuated the maldistribution of wealth) and by proponents of the business confidence thesis (who argued that it did havoc to normal economic expectations). It was denounced on the ground that it aggravated the disparity between agriculture and industry. It was seen by some as a "straitjacket" upon the American economy, freezing the status quo, preventing expansion. And it was assailed on all sides as monopolistic, an ideological schema which joined together those two American ogres—big business and big government.

ALTERNATIVES

Proposals mentioned as alternatives to or substitutes for the NRA approach included the Black shorter work week bill (especially in the context of 1933), later wage-and-hour legislation, the National Incorporation bill, and the Industrial Expansion bill (in 1937–38). Such alternatives were presented by proponents of the purchasing power thesis, who saw in them more effective routes to implementation of the thesis than that of NRA; by antimonopoly progressive opponents of the NRA; and by reluctant supporters of the NRA, who wanted to retain its planning features while rejecting its excessively probusiness orientation and its scarcity economics. Moreover, there were those, economic planners and natural recovery men alike, who particularly stressed the need for greatly increased productivity; to such men of both persuasions scarcity economics was hardly the road to reemployment and a higher standard of living.

One of the boldest thrusts along this last line came from Phil La Follette. Stressing the need for increased production, arguing that a more equitable distribution of an inadequate national income was of itself no solution, he attempted in 1938 to found a political party ideologically based upon the production expansion theme. He was not talking so much by 1937–38 in terms of the need to boost consumptive power; rather—for whatever reasons, political or otherwise—he was now stressing the theme of increased productivity per se. He declared in 1938, "We have tried to give the farmer high prices by restricting agricultural production. We have tried to give industry high prices by restricting . . . production. . . . We have tried to give labor high wages by restricting the output of the worker. . . . A little simple arithmetic gives the answer: *less* from agriculture, *less* from industry . . . , and *less* from labor. . . ."[42]

Max Lerner, analyzing La Follette's approach, wrote that it was, "in a way, the core of the National Expansion bill . . . introduced . . . by Amlie, Voorhis, and other progressives. . . . But Phil would not go as far as that bill in his program of regulation of industry."[43] Lerner's remark was to the point. Phil La Follette had never been a great enthusiast of economic planning. Whether through monetary manipulation, expanded exports, or increased production, he always seemed anxious to find some way around the more rigorous controls of a planned economy, to minimize direct government intervention in the processes of production. In this sense he reflected the general reluctance of American politicos to plan—even New Deal planners were generally reluctant planners—and the ever-present temptation to look elsewhere for "easier" cures to the economic crisis, cures more consistent with America's traditional ideological norms.

This factor—Phil La Follette's relative reluctance to plan—perhaps partially explains the reception a man like Josiah Bailey, a good conservative Democrat, could give to La Follette's speech launching the National Progressives of America. To be sure, Bailey was no doubt delighted to see an open political split on the left between the New Deal and La Follette progressivism—so there was a political rationale for his praise—yet it was also significant that he could find such clearly common ideological ground on which to stand with the progressive. Declared Bailey in 1938, "I am not surprised that the Progressives have struck the note of productivity as a means of recovery. . . . The Governor of Wisconsin, forming his new party, . . . repudiates coercion; he repudiates restriction of crops and says, 'Let the people go; let them produce; the only way . . . out of the depression is to create ever-increasing amounts of wealth.' I knew that before he said it. . . . I do not now mind approving it."[44]

The Industrial Expansion bill of 1937–38, based upon the proposals of New Deal economist Mordecai Ezekiel, supported by the House "mavericks" and cosponsored by Congressmen Maury Maverick, Jerry Voorhis, Tom Amlie, and Robert G. Allen, was expressly designed to expedite production through planning.[45] Legislatively it made no progress, yet ideologically it was symptomatic. In a 1938 statement the Maverick group (itself a potpourri of erstwhile socialists, "advanced" New Dealers, progressives, and radicals) urged such legislation in order "to bring about, through the cooperation of government, business, and labor, a coordinated expansion of industrial production and an effective control over . . . monopoly price increases and monopolistic curtailment of production. . . ."[46]

Jerry Voorhis provided the fullest exposition of the principles of the Industrial Expansion bill, and his arguments—meshing the planning philosophy with a version of antimonopolism—reflected the changed atmosphere of 1937–38. Voorhis argued that producers were reluctant to expand production when they did not know what producers in other lines were going to do and therefore whether there would be a market for increased output. He contended that to assure a market for increased production, producers in various lines of industry had to increase production simultaneously and the distribution of income had to be more equitable, with a larger share going to workers in wages or to consumers in lower prices and a smaller share going to profits. Better distribution alone would not suffice—increased production was also needed.[47]

The fundamental difficulty, as Voorhis saw it, lay in the pervasiveness of monopoly control. In industries under such control ample profits could be made through a policy of high prices and limited production. This, however, served to restrict purchasing power and lessen the market generally for the products of industry; the real need was for a policy of low prices and unlimited production, machinery to prevent higher prices from nullifying higher wages, and a "central plan" to provide for a coordinated increase of production in all major industries. "Already the broad outlines of this machinery have been suggested in the N.R.A. and the A.A.A. In both these cases, however, the method . . . was . . . a restriction of production down to the level of effective demand. Also the N.R.A. attempted to include too many small industries . . . which do not affect general economic conditions enough to require any sharp control over them."[48]

The Industrial Expansion bill would establish machinery to bring about "voluntary agreements" in the major industries to provide against price increases, to provide for coordinated production increases, and to provide for an equitable distribution of the income resulting from increased production, with a maximum of ten per cent allotted to profits and the remaining going to wages and (by way of lower prices) to consumers. The bill further "provided that all cooperating producing units are to be protected against loss from unsalable surpluses by means of government purchase of such surpluses . . . if . . . necessary. Practically, then, what our bill offers to industry is the removal of uncertainty with regard to markets." The "great question is this: If the . . . power of government can be used to adjust agricultural production, why cannot it be used to increase industrial production?"[49]

Other plans and proposals were offered, among them the National Incorporation bill designed to bar from interstate trade corporations engaged in unfair practices. Its two leading spokesmen were William Borah, who looked to it to meet the monopoly problem,[50] and Senator Joseph O'Mahoney. O'Mahoney argued that National Incorporation would provide an alternative both to the concentration of private economic power and to the expansion of federal bureaucracy, spur a fairer distribution of income, prevent manipulation of prices contrary to consumer interests, aid small business, and pave the way for recovery. It called for self-government in industry, and not for the harassing controls characteristic of NRA. "We don't need more regulation of business," O'Mahoney declared. "We need only to prevent abuses. . . . A [National Incorporation] law would not require an army of agents to enforce it. . . . It would be almost self-enforcing." It would provide a "really . . . competitive system."[51]

A shorter work week, often coupled with a call for higher wages—in other words, a specific program expressly designed to expand purchasing power—was a frequently proposed alternative. In the form of the 30-hour bill, it passed the Senate in 1933. Hugo Black, its foremost political proponent (and the 30-hour bill's sponsor), looked to it to provide a solution for technological unemployment as such, and by increasing employment and purchasing power to pave the way for general recovery.[52] The shorter work week had a further attraction in that it avoided resort to the rigors of economic planning and large-scale government intervention. As James Mead put it, the shorter work week's "simplicity recommends its application above every other device yet advocated. It necessitates no bureaucracy or governmental supervision."[53]

Proponents of the purchasing power thesis also looked to wage-and-hour legislation in 1937–38 to expand consumptive capacity. Franklin Roosevelt, for example, in April 1938 (employing a rationale much like that he had used in calling for the NIRA) asserted that "Competition, of course, like all other good things, can be carried to excess. . . . The exploitation of child labor, the chiseling of workers' wages, the stretching of workers' hours, are not . . . proper methods of competition. I have consistently urged a federal wages and hours bill to take the minimum decencies of life for the working man . . . out of the field of competition."[54] New Dealers Mead and James Murray both argued in 1938 that wage-and-hour legislation would expand purchasing power and expedite recovery.[55] Thus while the legislative proposals changed, from NRA to its alternatives, the underlying rationale remained essentially the same.

Prophets of abundance were heard from both right and left. To some increased production was an "easy" remedy which would avoid the rigors of planning; to others it could come only as a result of the "hard" remedy of planned reconstruction. Conservatives, of course, considered themselves the true prophets of abundance;   American capitalism, they argued, had achieved the greatest economy of plenty the world had ever known. Many progressives and New Dealers argued that Americans could consume far more than they were consuming, that implementation of the purchasing power thesis provided the necessary basis for this economy of abundance. And socialists and planned economy enthusiasts continually argued that the cooperative commonwealth would usher in an era of unparalleled abundance, that freed from the artificial restraints of an illogical capitalism America's productive capacity could be used to its full.

The Industrial Expansion bill was the leading planning proposal of 1937–38—a time when planning was a good deal less in vogue than in 1933. The plan was something of a hybrid, with diverse political and ideological roots. It could be traced in a broad and general sense to Thorstein Veblen; more immediately to Mordecai Ezekiel, of Henry Wallace's Department of Agriculture; and to the implications of studies of potential productive capacity conducted by the relatively orthodox Brookings Institution and the relatively radical ex-Technocrat Harold Loeb. The plan's sponsors included Maury Maverick, New Dealer from Texas; Jerry Voorhis, ex-Socialist and one-time supporter of Upton Sinclair's EPIC (End Poverty In California) campaign; and Tom Amlie, erstwhile advocate of public ownership and a distinctly American cooperative commonwealth.

The plan was designed to benefit from the experience of AAA and NRA, avoiding the latter's errors and spurring production and employment. It reflected the growing concern of New Dealers in the late thirties with the problem of administered prices; it was bound up with the New Deal's increasing acceptance of a low-price, mass volume economy as the way out of depression. It would be "AAA in reverse," using government to encourage expansion rather than contraction of production. It would not permit business control, but it would meet the business confidence argument. It would not take too many industries under its aegis like NRA, but it would (at least to an extent) meet the earlier radical criticism that the New Deal lacked a central, coordinating plan.

Antimonopoly progressives of the Borah-O'Mahoney stripe unsuccessfully advanced the National Incorporation measure, seeing in it a way to prevent both the concentration of private economic power and the expansion of federal bureaucracy. The shorter work week was likewise advanced as a way to avoid complicated structural schemes—such as the NRA. Finally, minimum wage-maximum hour legislation was successfully pushed by New Dealers as a means (like NRA in this regard) to eliminate "unfair" competitive practices and to implement the purchasing power thesis. Each of these alternatives, including the Industrial Expansion bill, lacked the grandiosity of planning schemes of 1933-34, schemes which reflected the short-lived epochal mood which (in intellectual more than political circles, to be sure) saw in "planning" the advent of a whole new socioeconomic era.

6

ECONOMIC SYSTEMS

The debate over economic "systems" had two main facets: first, the perennial competition-monopoly issue; and second, the larger controversy over what constituted a "system" and what the implications of the New Deal were in this context. The discussion of monopoly evidenced the strength of tradition, the impact by 1937–38 of traditional progressivism upon the New Deal, and the development of the administered prices concept in relation to the purchasing power thesis. The broader discussion of "systems" demonstrated further implications of the conservative critique of the New Deal, and illustrated the dogmatic quality of much of the argument of both left and right.

COMPETITION AND MONOPOLY

Calls for a return to competitive capitalism and attacks upon the menace of monopoly have echoed through decades of American history; like monetary formulae, they were part of an ancient tradition, enshrined in the American ethos. They were eclipsed somewhat by the early thirties vogue of planning and New Nationalist acceptance of large economic units (as opposed to New Freedomite antimonopolism, which was sometimes linked in the intellectual vogue to laissez-faire as an outdated doctrine of a by-gone era). Yet antimonopolism and calls for competition persisted even during this period, especially in the political arena, and they increased in appeal as planning declined, especially in 1937–38. Antimonopolism in the thirties, moreover, was directly related to the recovery question: for some, resolution of the monopoly problem was the key to implementation of the purchasing power thesis and the revival of national prosperity. Beyond this, arguments were advanced that monopoly threatened political democracy, and that it would end by provoking a reaction towards "state socialism."

William Borah, Joseph O'Mahoney, and Burt Wheeler were among the nation's leading antimonopoly spokesmen; these three progressives consistently sounded the antimonopoly theme through the years, well before it came back into full vogue in the late thirties. As Borah saw it, for example, monopoly was not the result of inexorable economic forces; if not arrested, it would lead to governmental regimentation; it could not be regulated, and had to be destroyed; it stifled "economic liberty" and imperiled political democracy.[1] O'Mahoney sought to avoid both private and public concentrations of power, arguing that the first was a sure road to the second. Great corporations, he contended, had grown too powerful; they had become "economic states"; they were not democratically responsible to the people. There could be no political liberty without economic freedom, and monopoly, public or private, was a threat to freedom.[2] Burt Wheeler contended that the concentration of economic power, private or public, involved regimentation, and that "private socialism" would end in government control and possibly a fascist state. The alternative was decentralization and renewed competition.[3]

Journalist Jonathan Mitchell noted in 1938 that William Borah and Robert Jackson "happen to be the two most conspicuous spokesmen in Washington against monopoly. . . ."[4] The comment was to the point. The progressive and the New Dealer agreed on monopoly's essential economic—and political—implications. (Burt Wheeler, too, in 1938 could declare himself in agreement with "Mr. Jackson's philosophy with reference to [monopoly]. . . .")[5] Jackson, the New Deal's leading antimonop-

oly spokesman in the later thirties, agreed with men like Borah,
Wheeler, and O'Mahoney, that "regimentation," be it public
or private, must be opposed, that a competitive economy pro-
vided the alternative to both big business and government control.
As Jackson once put it, "I do not think anybody disagrees with
Norman Thomas more than I do."[6]

Jackson argued that the choice in the final analysis lay between a competitive economy regulated by the antitrust laws and
a government-controlled economy; the people would not indefi-
nitely tolerate monopoly; "private socialism" would end in state
socialism. The economy could not remain "half monopoly and
half free competition." Concentrated private economic power was
not democratically responsible to the people, and could not effectively be regulated. It was a threat to political as well as to economic freedom. It destroyed enterprise. Big business which had
shown itself most efficient was not objectionable, but too many
oversized concerns were neither efficient nor dynamic. Government, accordingly, should act positively to promote competition.
"Governmental power to prevent concentration has not failed,"
Jackson concluded. "It has never been tried."[7]

A key argument dealt with the problem of monopoly price-
fixing. William Borah consistently sounded this theme—in his
critique of the NRA, in his analysis of the farm crisis, in his overall view of the economy. As Jonathan Mitchell wrote in 1936,
"Borah's indictment of monopoly . . . differs basically from the
nostalgic hankering for a return to a more primitive economic
system of the . . . 'Brandeis group' around Mr. Roosevelt. . . ."
Borah's critique of monopoly was central to his analysis of the
depression. He enthusiastically endorsed Gardiner Means's administered prices thesis. His views, moreover, expressed through
the thirties, presaged those which became increasingly influential
among New Dealers in 1937–38. The old progressive could declare
late in 1937, "I am in hearty accord with the views on monopoly
. . . expressed by Mr. [Robert] Jackson. . . . I can see no recovery
. . . so long as private interests fix prices and thereby continue to
deplete purchasing power."[8]

Borah considered monopoly prices the "most important" of
the depression's sources. He argued through these years that the

basic need was for expanded purchasing power and a more equitable distribution of income but that the inordinately high prices fixed by monopolies prevented satisfaction of this need by drawing off purchasing power into exorbitant profits, thereby preventing recovery. Monopoly prices stood between government and whatever good its spending could do by way of increasing purchasing power. Shorter hours and minimum wages would do little good given monopoly's power to fix the prices of what the worker had to buy. The need accordingly was to restore a truly competitive economy; this would break down monopoly prices, free the flow of purchasing power, and revive the economy.[9]

Burt Wheeler also argued in this vein, contending that while some prices, such as the farmer's, fell as the depression deepened, others, "administered" by industrial managers, remained rigid, causing production and employment to drop in their stead. This destroyed the market as a regulatory mechanism, upset the economy's equilibrium, curtailed purchasing power and consumption, and prevented readjustment and recovery. If capitalism was to survive prices had to be reduced to a point where people could buy; the need was for a return to price competition. Wheeler in a remarkable speech early in 1935 (which in many ways—point for point—anticipated Franklin Roosevelt's major antimonopoly pronouncement of April 1938) endorsed Gardiner Means's administered prices concept, and made it clear that the problem went beyond moralism: ". . . today we are forced to face, for purely economic reasons, a problem . . . of the inherent significance of corporate size as bearing upon the effective functioning of our economy. . . ."[10]

The progressive antimonopoly analysis clearly had implications that cohered with the planning philosophy. Yet, given the progressives' strong adherence to traditional dogma, their solution was a more limited one. Senator O'Mahoney, for example, argued that the depression persisted because large corporations refused to lower prices, thereby causing production, employment, purchasing power, and consumption to fall. But as O'Mahoney saw it, "production and employment, once released from the grasp of monopoly, will operate under the American system to distribute wealth among the masses in a perfectly natural and healthful manner."[11] The system itself, in other words, was deemed fundamentally sound—if only monopoly were removed from it. The latter was not viewed as a logical consequence of the processes of the former, but as something external and alien to it. Thus while the progressives' analyses could be sharp—and there were few political leaders during the thirties who were more astute in this regard than William Borah—their analyses ran beyond their solutions.

The administered prices concept, and the demand for a low price-high wage-mass volume mode of production as a way to implement the purchasing power thesis, came into vogue among New Dealers particularly during the 1937–38 recession. Like the progressives, they were influenced by Gardiner Means's 1935 analysis, *Industrial Prices and Their Relative Inflexibility;*[12] the work of an economic planner, it was employed to bolster the case for the antimonopoly rationale. The administered prices thesis was invoked during this period in the economic analyses of such New Dealers as Alben Barkley, James Mead, James Pope, and James Murray.[13] Murray, indicating another source of this approach, added that "The Brookings Institution has made a study . . . and has arrived at the conclusion that the . . . road to prosperity . . . is for corporations to allow wages to be raised without raising prices, and . . . that . . . only in that way, are we going to have prosperity. . . ."[14]

Robert Jackson in 1937 and 1938, of course, was one of the New Deal's leading exponents of the administered prices thesis, repeatedly arguing that rigid monopoly prices created a disequilibrium in the economy, depleting purchasing power, reducing labor's payroll, and preventing recovery. As an alternative, as a way to effect the purchasing power thesis, he called for positive government action to encourage a low price-high wage-high volume economy.[15] Robert Wagner, too, in 1938 (expressing agreement with Senator Borah) voiced dismay at the disparity between increases in prices and profits, on the one hand, and wages, on the other. He strongly supported the proposal for a study of monopoly by the Temporary National Economic Committee because of this concern.[16] (Discussion of the monopoly problem in the Senate often came down to a continuing dialogue between Wagner and Borah, with the New Dealer—and erstwhile advocate of the NRA—drawing closer and closer to the progressive's position as the years passed.)

Franklin Roosevelt's concern about excessively high prices in some industrial lines antedated the 1937 downturn, and he repeatedly argued during the recession that high rigid monopoly prices were curtailing employment, purchasing power, and production, that they were preventing recovery, and that the real need was for a low price-high volume economy.[17] At a 1937 press conference, he declared that steel prices were too high. A reporter queried whether any thought had been given "to trying to check that," to which the President replied: "I wish you would show me a way of doing it." Asked at a 1938 press conference whether he had a solution to the problem of undue price increases, he responded: "Unfortunately, not. . . . We were working towards it . . . in an experimental way under NRA. . . . At the present time the whole thing is being started anew, not with any thought . . . of reconstituting NRA. It is being started anew through the study of the . . . monopoly problem. . . ." The problem, apparently, in FDR's own terms, was as perplexing in 1938 as it was in 1933.[18]

For the problem here, as elsewhere, was how to institutionalize the purchasing power thesis (and remove the barriers to it) without transcending the bounds of the New Dealers' concept of capitalism. Roosevelt was well aware of the difficulties involved in trying to prevent monopoly price-fixing within the bounds of that concept of capitalism, but he never found a solution to them. Norman Thomas, on the other hand, focused on the same problem, but drew a definite conclusion as he criticized the low price-high volume rationale from a Socialist's perspective: "According to the experts of the Brookings Institution, the hope for the future of capitalism in America is to have an increase of production . . . with a low price level but high wages. When capitalism does that it ought to be easy for mathematicians to square the circle."[19]

The major arguments against monopoly—that it was inefficient and undynamic, that it could not be effectively regulated, that it constituted a kind of private socialism which would end in state socialism, that it was not democratically responsible to the people, that it posed a threat to political as well as to economic freedom—were sounded first by progressives such as Borah and Wheeler and only later, particularly in 1937–38, incorporated in a major way into the philosophy of the New Deal. Antimonopoly in the thirties had several sources: it was part of an ancient tradition, it reflected the reaction against NRA, it was a recoil against the rise of authoritarian collectivism in Europe. "Modern European history," Robert Jackson declared, "teaches us that free enterprise cannot exist alongside of monopolies and cartels."[20] Antimonopolists stressed their equal opposition to industrial and governmental "regimentation." They looked to a competitive economy—if need be, one in which competition was compelled by government—as the alternatives to both.

Most directly related to the problem of recovery was the question of monopoly price-fixing. Here, too, New Dealers by 1937–38 incorporated into their analyses an argument which progressives such as Borah and Wheeler had propounded through the decade. This theme was given a more sophisticated statement in 1935 by Gardiner Means, whose ideas found their way into the progressives' and New Dealers' antimonopoly programs. The crux of the administered prices thesis was that large industrial concerns, when faced with a falling demand, cut production and employment rather than prices, thereby further curtailing consumption and purchasing power, while other prices—such as agriculture's—remained flexible and fell. The basic alternative offered to this half monopoly-half market structure was the idea of a low price-high volume economy, a proposal developed in the 1936 Brookings Institution study *The Recovery Problem in the United States*. Its proponents argued that high wages and low prices would expand purchasing power, production, and consumption, while ensuring adequate profits through increased sales.

The administered prices concept provided yet another example of a New Deal-progressive analysis going beyond New Deal-progressive programs. The analysis (as a corollary of the purchasing power thesis) opened the door to various programs, including planning and public ownership, but the solution advanced was usually the thoroughly traditional one of a return to a competitive economy. Part of the problem here lay in the fact that the administered prices concept came into vogue among New Dealers only after the planning philosophy had come into disrepute. Part of the problem lay in the ideological blinders of the New Dealers themselves. In either case, the New Deal did not try to use the popular rhetoric of antimonopolism to advance the philosophy of economic planning, to fuse antimonopoly, planning, the administered prices concept, and the low price-high wage-mass volume formula into a viable and realistic politico-economic program.

"Competition" was a good, orthodox American concept which, for all the talk of "planning" in 1933–34, and for all the association in those NRA years of competition with "unfair" and predatory practices (though even here the objective held up was that of "fair" competition), could be espoused and apotheosized by everyone but the radicals—by New Dealers, progressives, and conservatives alike. For New Dealers, perplexed by the results of NRA, frustrated by the recession, the cry of antimonopoly had a familiar ring; so, too, did the call for a return to competition. The more radical implications and applications of antimonopolism were rejected or ignored. If in 1933 it had seemed that an era had come to an end, then by 1937 the epochal mood of the early thirties had clearly receded; competition had returned in all its glory to the American pantheon.

THE BROADER CONTROVERSY

The debate over economic "systems" was rooted in ideological tradition. The overall conservative view was essentially based upon a series of assumptions about government, society, and the economy derived from classical nineteenth-century liberalism. The New Deal position had intellectual roots in the reanalyses of classical liberalism of the late nineteenth century and of the progressive era. These philosophical suppositions in turn shaped or influenced particular policies; they perhaps played their largest and clearest role in 1933–34 when the "end of an era" atmosphere was strong, when the aura of crisis was greatest. Conservatives, in a world beset by a rise of autocratic systems, looked at the New

Deal's early NRA-AAA schema and saw European-style autocracy. New Dealers looked at their programs as alternatives to the extremes of both left and right.

To men bred in American traditions of individualism, witnessing the rise of fascism and autocracy abroad, the New Deal could well seem a revolutionary departure; dire portents could be seen in even the most modest of domestic policies and programs. John Taber, for example, argued that if minimum wages and maximum hours were fixed by government, then soon all wages would be so fixed, and private enterprise would cease, and "this . . . means . . . a totalitarian state. . . ."[21] Frank Knox contended that the New Deal was patterned on the model of planned economy, and that the price of planned economy was political autocracy. The Guffey coal bill, he asserted, contained "the precise doctrine enunciated by . . . Mussolini. . . ." It was "pure Fascist economics!"[22] Alf Landon warned against government dictation and regimentation, arguing that it characterized the New Deal, and that "planned economy" was incompatible with liberty and democracy.[23]

Such leading conservative spokesmen as Herbert Hoover, Ogden Mills, and Lewis Douglas joined in the refrain that the New Deal imposed collectivism, and that it placed America on the road to the totalitarian state. Hoover argued that the New Dealers were set upon creating a regimented economic order which would obstruct the operation of free enterprise by mixing socialism, fascism, and collectivism into the American system.[24] Mills denounced the scarcity system of "bureaucratic . . . regimentation," insisting that the New Deal partook of the same collectivist philosophy as fascism and communism. Planned economy eroded the dynamism of free enterprise, he argued, and inevitably ended in complete regimentation.[25] Collectivism, Douglas contended, was incompatible with democratic processes and a free society; it was a scarcity system; it would end in political autocracy, a static society, permanent unemployment.[26]

Douglas and Newton Baker argued that New Deal regimentation was an offshoot of the New Era of the twenties. The New Era subsidized private monopoly; the New Deal subsidized other economic groups, and created state-sanctioned monopolies; a threat to liberty inhered in both.[27] The need, Douglas argued, was for a truly competitive system without artificial mechanisms. The New Era did not constitute such a system. It was a modern imitation of the seventeenth-century pattern, complete with high tariffs and government-sanctioned price-fixing.[28] John W. Davis attacked President Hoover for taking the country down the road to socialism—and then commenced a like attack upon the New Deal's road to "state capitalism."[29] Conservative Democrat Albert Ritchie, too, assailed the expansion of government's economic role under both Hoover and Roosevelt.[30] And Congressman James Beck deemed the New Deal's economic controls only a continuation of the dire trend begun under Hoover.[31]

". . . the New Deal," Frank Knox declared, "is essentially a Tory movement. . . ." Knox[32] and others went beyond this to contend that the New Deal was profoundly reactionary, an attempt to regress, to reinstitute an economic philosophy antedating the industrial revolution. "The . . .'New Deal,' " James Beck insisted, "is not new. . . . It has been tried in all ages . . . and has always led to disaster."[33] Senator Roscoe Patterson asserted that the New Deal's program "is not . . . progressive. . . . It is reactionary. It turns the clock of progress back thousands of years. It is an assault on human liberty."[34] William H. King argued that present economic policy was a reversion to ancient and feudal times, to the "Dark Ages," when economic and political life was controlled by arbitrary authority, against which the people ultimately revolted to establish systems of economic and political liberty.[35]

Ogden Mills argued that planned economy was not new; it was as old as Rome, existed in the Middle Ages, and was almost universal prior to the nineteenth century; under it "economic progress was measured in terms of centuries rather than decades"; it had been tried throughout history and had always failed. It was the very system against which the founding fathers revolted. It involved an authoritarian state, a scarcity economy, a static society. It was the philosophy underlying the New Deal. With planned economy, Mills declared, "The United States is to be transformed into a sort of Spain of the sixteenth century."[36]

Herbert Hoover compared NRA codes to the "guild monop-

olies . . . in the Elizabethan period, from which we derived much
of our American antagonism to monopoly." American liberties
were born in rebellion against economic tyranny. The philosophy
of economic regimentation was not new; it existed in other societies and in earlier ages. Declared Hoover, "A 'reactionary' in
ordinary times is a gentleman who wants to re-establish the *status
quo ante*. The New Deal wants to do precisely that—as a matter
of fact it is *status quo George III* or *Diocletian*." Under collectivism "the people find they are marching backwards toward the
Middle Ages—as regimented men."[37]

Such conservative critics argued that the New Deal was
abandoning the very economic system which had produced the
greatest prosperity the world had ever known, the very economic
system which was indeed inseparable from economic progress.
Alf Landon, for example, argued that unlike other countries,
where governmental bureaucracy had restricted economic freedom, "the American way . . . has left men . . . free from these
restrictions. . . . Under this encouragement, business has expanded
here faster than elsewhere. . . ."[38] Herbert Hoover argued that a
free economy alone provided those stimuli to creative human im-
pulses essential to economic progress and plenty.[39] As Lewis
Douglas saw it, "It has been . . . individual man's creative gen-
ius, set free and compelled to operate by the momentum of . . .
competitive forces, which has raised us up out of the slough of
the Middle Ages. . . ."[40]

The American system, as Ogden Mills conceived it, was one
of economic liberalism, dependent upon the creative energies of
free men, with government regulation to ensure competition.
Only such an economy could provide abundance. It had provided decades of ever-increasing prosperity up to the World War
and the depression; it operated with equipoise and efficiency; it
stimulated new inventions and economic progress. What, Mills
asked, unleashed the great economic progress of the century before 1914? Technological development? If so, why was there
technological development after so many centuries of stagnation?
The answer was "freedom." Technological advance came in
those countries—America and Britain—where economic freedom
was greatest.[41]

It was commonly asserted (by those to the left as well as to the right of the New Deal) that any attempt to mix the traditional American economic system with socialism or planned economy would not work. The choice had to be one—or the other; there could be no mixed economy partaking of elements of both. There could be no permanent reconstruction between the extremes; the New Deal's effort to fashion a "middle way" could not endure; the road away from capitalism, once embarked upon, had no stopping point short of a wholly new economic system. Conservatives advancing in this vein included Hoover, Vandenberg, Mills, Landon, Knox, and Josiah Bailey.[42] "Once we abandon the voluntary principles," Bailey declared, "we run squarely into Communism. . . . There can be no half-way control."[43] On the left, Communist Earl Browder, EPIC leader Upton Sinclair, and native American radical Tom Amlie all advanced versions of the "either-or" theme.[44]

Another common argument was that economic and political liberty were inseparable, capitalism and democracy inextricable, that if the one was lost the other was sure to follow. Conservatives Hoover, Mills, Landon, Bailey, and Knox all argued in this vein.[45] As Lewis Douglas put it, "if a planned economy is to be attempted . . . all of our cherished liberties, freedom of speech, freedom of the press, political freedom, our representative form of government, must be abandoned." It meant "dictatorship."[46] Progressives advanced a version of this theme in an antimonopoly-antibureaucracy context; and New Dealers also proceeded along these lines. James Murray, for example, argued in 1938 that the New Deal "saved our capitalistic system . . . and in saving capitalism it . . . saved democracy."[47] And Franklin Roosevelt declared in 1936 that "Private enterprise is necessary to any Nation which seeks to maintain the democratic form of government."[48]

Conservatives tended to think in terms of economic "systems"; American capitalism must be kept inviolate; any admixture of alien isms was forbidden. Edgar Kemler remarked in 1941 that the conservatives during the thirties were "the real perfectionists," they were "now the dreamers and the Utopians."[49] John Taber and Al Smith both based their thirties criticisms upon fixed ideas and assumptions antedating the depression.[50] Carter Glass, Lewis Douglas, and Herbert Hoover were all intellectually rigid and dogmatic. Hoover, to be sure, was willing to use the government to meet the economic crisis; as President, he did so use it. But with his rigid categorization of economic systems he insisted that any extension of government beyond a certain point (the point to which he himself was willing to go) threatened the American system, and therefore recovery, democracy, liberty, and the nation's way of life.[51]

Franklin Roosevelt, too, for all of his genuine open-mindedness, also adhered to certain assumptions, which were none the less binding for being relatively unsystematized, and which blunted his pragmatism and limited his propensity to experiment. While by no means as rigid as Hoover, his difference with his predecessor was in this respect perhaps more one of degree than of kind. He was unable critically to contemplate more drastic alternatives than those he actually espoused.[52] As Rex Tugwell put it, "In spite of his inquiring mind and experimental temper, the inquiring and the experimentation were still confined—and rather strictly . . . —within old boundaries. . . ." ". . . Franklin remained within this [traditional] ideological pattern all his life. He would strain it on occasion, but not severely. Its hold on his mind would never be loosened."[53]

New Dealers not infrequently reacted to proposals more radical than their own in much the same way that conservatives reacted to New Deal programs; they denounced them as contrary to American traditions and divined in them dangerous implications. Roosevelt, for example, discussing more radical alternatives, sometimes sounded like Herbert Hoover denouncing the New Deal. He declared that "Any paternalistic system which tries to provide security for everyone from above only calls for an impossible task and a regimentation utterly uncongenial to the spirit of our people." At a 1937 press conference he was asked whether the railroads should be subsidized. "Why railroads?," answered the President. "Why not the cotton mills? Why not everything else? You are working toward state socialism."[54]

Roosevelt once very eloquently declared that "the New

Deal ... is working out ... current problems from day to day as necessities arise and with whatever materials are at hand. We are doing this without attempting to commit the Nation to any ism or any ideology except democracy, humanity and the civil liberties which form their foundations."[55] But a Norman Thomas comment was to the point: "... President Roosevelt ... has a tendency toward an open mind and is willing to experiment, but he always oscillates on the same plane."[56] Not only a Robert Jackson, but also a Franklin Roosevelt and such New Deal planners as Wallace and Wagner had ideological commitments beyond those to "democracy, humanity and civil liberties," and argued against more pervasive planning in much the same terms that conservatives criticized their own New Deal experiments.

In the world of the thirties, replete with fascism and autocracy, many American conservatives, as liberals of the classical persuasion, divined in the New Deal portents of European collectivism and regimentation. As Amos Pinchot warned the President, "What has happened in Europe makes it clear ... that, if a leader pursues the path of bureaucratic regimentation of industry and agriculture, he must go forward into dictatorship, whether he wants to or not. ..."[57] Such men feared that the New Deal was a revolutionary departure from American traditions of economic and political freedom, that it was rejecting the very free economy that had made possible the nation's great economic progress, that it was ignoring the axiom that (in the words of Herbert Hoover) "the source of economic prosperity is freedom."[58]

Many critics of this variety, defenders (as they saw themselves) of liberal political and economic institutions against autocratic collectivism, argued that the New Deal was in fact profoundly reactionary, an attempt to restore the forms of economic authoritarianism against which America's founding fathers had revolted, an attempt to return to the "planned economy" of mercantilism, of the Middle Ages, of ancient times—systems which had suppressed individual rights, required political autocracy, retarded economic progress, and resulted in scarcity economies and static societies. It was only with the eighteenth- and nineteenth-century reaction against these systems, they asserted, and the creation of free institutions, that human freedom and economic progress flowered and flourished; it was only with its free economy that America became such a superb example of economic prosperity and progress.

A common idea, advanced by both conservatives and radicals, was that economic "systems" could not be mixed, that the nation could have capitalism, or it could have socialism, but it could not have a successful mixture of the two in terms either of particular policies or permanent reconstruction. Another common idea, popular among conservatives, but also advanced in New Deal-progressive versions, was that economic and political freedom, private enterprise and democratic government, were inseparable. In its conservative version, this was a restatement of the thesis that planned economy led to political autocracy; in its progressive version it partook of antimonopolism (and antibureaucracy); in its New Deal version it revealed a deep underlying commitment to the political implications of capitalist folklore.

Many conservatives—Herbert Hoover was a prime example —argued that the government could go just so far in the economic realm; and to go any further would open the door to regimentation, fascism, and autocracy. But New Dealers and progressives, too, while certainly more open to experiment than the conservatives, nonetheless also failed either to apply their pragmatism to an analysis of the economy as a whole, or warned (à la Hoover) of the dire implications involved in proposals and programs more radical than their own. For progressives and New Dealers, as well as for conservatives, this dogmatic mode of thinking proved restrictive in the search for concrete solutions to deal with very practical problems; for progressives and New Dealers, as well as for conservatives, it illustrated the doctrinaire limits of the American ideological tradition.

7

THE RECOVERY DEBATE
An Appraisal

The key division of the debate came over the origins of the depression, and the consequent—and centrally conflicting—confidence and purchasing power theses. This division, and these theses, had broader implications—social and political, as well as ideological. Certain themes which cut across the debate, appearing in discussions of various subjects, were most revelatory of the character of the debate itself—and therefore of the nature of the American ideological tradition. These themes also had their broader implications.

THE PRIMARY DIVIDE

The division over the historical roots of the depression served to separate many New Dealers, modern progressives, and radicals from conservatives of the thirties on a whole range of key issues. While there were points of convergence between all these groups on various questions, this division—linked to the related division over the purchasing power and confidence theses—caused cleavages which in the context of the time seemed unbridgeable. The very policies which one group saw as vital to meet the new needs of the mature economy, the other group saw as the preventives of the "natural" recovery of a still vital American capitalism which did not now revive only because of the faulty assumptions of the New Deal as to the depression's causes and to the consequent New Deal policies.

While the economic maturity thesis thus served fundamentally to divide radicals and (less inclusively) New Dealers and progressives from conservatives, the differing radical and New Deal-progressive interpretations of the thesis provided bases for very fundamental divisions between them. Should the existing system in which the reformers had faith and wished to retain on grounds apart from economic maturity be reordered and restabilized? Various progressives and New Dealers, after all, saw the alternative—"socialism"—as the road to dictatorship and incompatible with the New Deal-progressive, much less the conservative version of the "middle way." Or should the existing system be discarded for a new one? Radicals favored this course on grounds apart from the economic maturity thesis, regarding capitalism as they did as a pernicious and exploitative system.

While New Dealers, progressives, and radicals differed with conservatives on the past role of the western frontier, one group considering it the key to an understanding of the historic path of American capitalism and the other denying it, they also differed on what the "new" frontier should be, conservatives relying upon their traditional and continuing dependence on the scientific frontier, and New Dealers, progressives, and radicals looking to government economic intervention as their version of a nongeographic frontier. For the conservatives, then, their rejection of the key role of the geographic frontier and their emphasis on both the historic and present importance of the scientific frontier provided continuity to their views of the American economy and society and provided a bridge between their past and present economic policies and programs.

The mature economy thesis thus not only provided a basis for a shift of those on the reformist left toward increased government economic intervention, but also provided a sharp divider which wrenched apart the degree of ideological homogeneity between reformers and conservatives that (at least in terms of the New Deal-progressive view of the historic role of the frontier) had existed in the past on the self-adjusting nature of American capitalism, or at least on the ability of American capitalism to adjust without great governmental intervention. This was true even though New Dealer-progressives and conservatives differed in their present views of what had in the past made capitalism able to adjust, one group pointing to the external impact of expanding geographic frontiers, and the other stressing the beneficent role of science and technology and arguing in any case that the self-adjustment was largely inherent in the very processes of the system.

If private investment and willingness to invest was a vital —the vital—ingredient in the dynamism of American capitalism, then the La Follette brothers' version of the implications of the frontier thesis—that real incentive for private investment no longer existed—could well seem crucial. If private investors could no longer provide this key function, then the government must. Was this still capitalism? Private ownership would remain, but control and key functions would move more and more to public hands by the very logic of the assumptions. Was it socialism? There would be no actual public ownership of key industries, and the powers government utilized would be its historic ones, such as fiscal policy. It would be a kind of hybrid system, incorporating ingredients of both the old capitalism and the new imperatives brought on by the needs (in this view) of the mature economy.

This provides a basis for understanding how conservatives could regard this hybrid (or New Deal) economy as the road to socialism. Was not government now assuming the historic and fundamental functions of private investors? And it provides a basis for understanding how radicals could regard the New Deal economy as essentially capitalism, or "state capitalism." Private ownership remained, great corporations remained in private hands, only now the state actively and directly intervened to prop up the processes of the continuing capitalist system. In one view, then, the New Deal could be seen as destructive of capitalism, and in the other as capitalism's very (though necessarily temporary) preservative. Thus the ideological basis of the hybrid sheds light on how men could take such different views of its nature—socialism in one view, continued capitalism in the other.

There were uses, political and otherwise, in finding past precedents for present policies, in presenting policies as just as fundamentally rooted in American traditions as any others. The New Deal version of a government-subsidized economic past— free lands as government's historic intervention in the economy —combined the view that the frontier had provided a basis for the self-adjusting capitalism of the past and the implication that the frontier's disappearance provided a dual justification for the government's intervention in the present. If the frontier had provided a basis for a self-adjusting capitalism in the past, it was because government had acted to use free lands to this end. In this sense the frontier thesis was used in two ways: as a basis for government intervention because the frontier had disappeared, and as a precedent for government intervention because of the way the free lands of the frontier had been used to sustain capitalism in the past.

Acceptance of the idea that capitalist prosperity in the past had *always* been sustained by government meant that prosperity had always been "artificial" as measured against conservative standards—not only with the foreign loans of the twenties, or the spending of the thirties, but always. The economic maturity thesis, government intervention, and artificial prosperity were thus linked. If government intervention and external forces had staved off the great depression through such undesirable measures as war spending and foreign loans, then the question became not *whether* government should act to sustain the economy but *how* it should act—by destructive devices, by wars, or by measures designed to improve the quality of American life, to lift the living standards of the people, to meet the challenges of poverty and social injustice, to "build up America."

Conservatives argued that the economic maturity theme was a gauge of the pessimism of the decade, and there was a measure of truth to this regardless of the theme's accuracy as a gauge of economic realities. The decade could appear to many to be a watershed, a period of epochal change; drastic alterations were taking place abroad; societies, economies, governments, and traditional values of the nineteenth-century mold were under attack; fascism and communism seemed threats to the very bases of western civilization as seen by Americans of many persuasions. In a period characterized by continuing depression, massive unemployment, the seeming collapse of the international structure of nineteenth-century capitalism, the contagion of autarchy, a slackening population growth rate, and a general vogue and atmosphere that the end of an era was at hand, the mature economy theme seemed to make sense.

Conservatives, of course, seemed immune to much of this, their faith in American capitalism firm and unshaken. Two factors stood out here: first, this showed to some extent the rigidity, persistent patterns, and unchanging or slowly changing quality of American ideology, especially in a popular or political context. Second, it illustrated the limited extent to which some of the intellectual vogues of the period penetrated into the political realm, not affecting—or influencing to a relatively marginal extent—the ideas and attitudes of most political leaders. This further illustrated the divide between intellectual and political life in America, the lack of intellectuals among politicians, and the politicos's tendency to remain affixed to ancient dogmas. This was a question of degree, of course, yet the continuity of ideas and attitudes in the intellectual history of American politics was clear.

The conservatives' confidence thesis was striking in the sense that it cohered so completely with what business considered to be its own interests. It had no real agricultural application; it provided no direct appeal to farmers' any more than to workers' interests. Conservatives, when appealing to farmers, usually spoke in terms that did not centrally flow from their basic confidence thesis; they spoke of trade policy, criticized crop control, but as a unit presented no single cohesive alternative. The confidence thesis entered into conservatives' agricultural appeals indirectly in the sense that they argued that a revival of industrial prosperity would ensure a better home market for farmers. Conservatives could appeal to workers as well as to farmers in at least this indirect way, arguing that farmer-worker interests would be benefited in the end through implementation of the thesis (thereby presenting a conservative version of the concept of economic interdependence—in this case, really *dependence*—which New Dealers stressed so much).

The cleavage between the confidence thesis and the purchasing power thesis may not at a voting group level support Arthur Schlesinger, Jr.'s idea that the political and social struggle in America can best be understood as a conflict between the business community (as the strongest group) and other groups in the society, but at an ideological level the basic breakdown was along such lines. The confidence thesis focused on the needs of business, and through the satisfaction of those needs, the interests of others. The purchasing power thesis had a wider interest base of appeal, stressing the direct needs not of business but of farmers, workers, and at a rhetorical level, "the people," and stressing—unlike the confidence thesis—that business interests could best be served by satisfaction of "the people's" interests and not vice versa.

The confidence thesis was further related to the whole question of power in a democracy. Conservatives criticized planned economy on the ground that it would place great power in the hands of a few men, yet their own confidence thesis rested the economic life of a nation and its people on the "confidence," on the psychological state, of a small part of that people and that nation. Granting for the moment the validity of the conservatives' assumption that planned economy would end in autocracy, one can nonetheless ask whether their own cherished system was any more democratic than their version of planned economy as measured by their own standards. The people's political representatives could be elected and defeated; but how directly responsive could business leaders and investors be to popular wishes, especially when, as conservatives would have it, political "interference" in business processes by the people's elected representatives would impair confidence, halt investment, and bring economic ruin?

Conservatives, granting their assumptions, did discuss in a systematic and comprehensive way why the depression persisted after 1932. But unlike New Dealers, progressives, and radicals, who argued back upon the twenties from the ruin of 1929 and contended that the prosperity of previous years in one sense or another, due to foreign loans, or glossed-over income maldistribution, or to the persisting farm depression, had been "artificial" and doomed therefore to collapse, conservatives (especially GOP conservatives who could not, like many conservative Democrats, point to the foreign economic policies of the twenties as lying behind the crisis) had difficulties in explaining the depression. They could point to the World War, but their logic was fuzzy as to how the destruction of the war could lead to the crash a decade later following a period of apparently unparalleled prosperity. They could say that the New Deal stopped the upturn of 1932, yet many found this too convenient an explanation.

The conservatives had a single coherent underlying philosophy which shaped, ordered, and lent consistency to their particular views. They had in the confidence-natural recovery thesis an inclusive general theory of how the economy worked. The purchasing power thesis similarly provided an underlying rationale for many proposals. But while New Dealers, progressives, and radicals all agreed that the thesis pinpointed the basic problem— income maldistribution, they sharply differed as to whether the thesis should be implemented through limited planning, antimonopoly, socialism, or some other formula. Similarly, the wide base of support for the purchasing power thesis at the theoretical level could become fractured at the programmatic level. The vague concept of economic interdependence notwithstanding, in the New Deal schema of ill-coordinated programs there remained a conflict as to whether the stress on purchasing power thesis implementation should be placed upon measures most directly and immediately beneficial to farmers, workers, or consumers.

Many New Dealers, moreover, as well as a socialist like Norman Thomas, argued that the Roosevelt administration had not adequately met the need for income redistribution; here both New Dealers and radicals could agree as to the inadequacy of the New Deal effort to save capitalism from itself, to redistribute income in order to keep the system going. Where they differed was in their assumptions, the New Dealers believing that in time it could be done and capitalism could be saved, and a Thomas unconvinced of both. So while they agreed on the short-range failure, they disagreed on the possibilities of long-range success; and their disagreement, of course, was in turn based upon their underlying assumptions about the possibilities of saving the system. Radicals could argue that all sorts of programs suggested by reformist supporters of the purchasing power thesis could be adopted without solving the problem; they could affect the economy, but they would not alter the framework of fundamental control; they could not provide an overall mechanism to keep income properly balanced and the economy functioning smoothly; they were no substitute for the fundamental changes that would be brought by public ownership and central planning.

The purchasing power thesis in its New Deal application was part of the Roosevelt administration's particular "middle way" between pre-1929 capitalism and out-and-out socialism, and structurally can best be understood in this context. It was the path which would save the system from itself; it would involve a degree of government intervention that was anathema to old-line conservatives, but it would steer away from the vagaries of pure socialism. Its very middle nature—more government intervention than before yet not so much as a Norman Thomas would want, government intervention in the name of saving the system yet government intervention which the system's more traditionally-minded adherents thought would destroy it—helps explain why some could denounce the New Deal as a state capitalism of the right while others could assault it as a socialism of the left, how some could view it as a last-ditch effort to preserve existing processes, and others could denounce it as a radical departure from those very processes.

THE DEFINING CHARACTERISTICS

The characteristic themes which cut across the discussion included the emergency rationale, balance, antiplanning, artificial prosperity, and pragmatism. Various New Deal programs—including public spending and crop control—were presented by their proponents as emergency solutions designed to meet crisis conditions. America must ultimately choose, the refrain ran, but for the moment it could rely upon such emergency expedients as provided by pump priming, production restriction plans, and so forth. Once the crises passed, these various arguments went, once business revived, once the agricultural export trade was spurred, once the world trend toward autarchy was reversed, these programs could be replaced by more permanent and orthodox formulae. The emergency motif sprang in part from the fact that there *were* emergency conditions which required quick remedies. But the programs stuck after the emergency passed; it was an era of emergency programs awaiting the reestablishment of a norm that never came. When crop control was curtailed another agricultural surplus crisis ensued; when spending was cut back a severe recession followed.

The quest for balance constituted another central theme. Often spoken of as a New Deal concept, it in fact had no necessary ideological anchor, and entered into virtually all programs and all rationales. Proponents of the purchasing power thesis, for example, focused on the disequilibrium inherent in the gap between productive and consumptive capacity. Planners urged that the chaos of unregulated capitalism be replaced with a coordinated economy. Foes of planning charged that it was government intervention which prevented the self-adjusting economy from returning to a state of equipoise. The balance rationale was used in attacks upon monopoly, which, it was charged, through price-fixing and the elimination of competition, created distortions and disparities in the economy. The concept lay at the very heart of the farm problem, the disparity between industry and agriculture. And it was used as a rationale for the money cure, for "reflation" to facilitate debt payment.

The concept of balance went to the core of a central question of the thirties: could the New Deal work? Could it create a balanced economy? Or would it, as adherents of classical capitalism and classical socialism alike argued, merely move from improvisation to improvisation, from expedient to expedient, from chaos to chaos? The concept also had more subtle uses: while the calls for "planning" and "balance" often went together, the balance concept sometimes came to the fore where the planning concept might have been expected. The idea of balance, after all, was capable of being meshed into just about any ideological schema—including that of the conservative anti-planners—and the concept could perhaps be used in place of the more drastic concept of planning (as calls for emergency programs could be substituted for calls for permanent formulae) by American political leaders reluctant to go outside the nation's traditional ideological frame; unlike planning it could easily be espoused and accepted within that frame. And the concept of balance, moreover, could be expressed even more vaguely than the concept of planning.

A leading rationale advanced by varied spokesmen for particular programs was that their scheme would avoid noisome planning, "bureaucracy," and "regimentation," that it would restore the economy without the irksome interferences of NRAs and AAAs. National Incorporation and McNary-Haugenism were advanced as remedies that would avoid the resort to bureaucratic controls. Proponents of the business confidence-natural recovery thesis, of course, posed their case in these terms, and they were often joined by export trade and currency expansion enthusiasts. All were offered as relatively simple solutions which, without structural change or extensive planning, would restore the economy. (This was implicit in spending as well; the fiscal cure was basically external, requiring no major alteration within the economy. But it was seldom made explicit, perhaps because supporters usually conceived of spending in purely emergency and expediential terms.)

Other examples may be cited. Some farm state men argued that agricultural recovery, like monetary reform or exports expansion, would do away with any need for government controls and artificial schemes in industry which were outside the bounds of the "American way." The 30-hour week could similarly be supported in terms of the degree to which it did not depart from traditional formulae, and the degree to which it did not move toward planned economy. It was a simple change, not involving the complex of institutional readjustments of a truly planned economy. It was—to borrow a monetary example—like currency expansion in that it was resigned to break the logjam without changing the fundamental institutional arrangements of the system; it was akin in this sense to other measures mentioned as alternatives to extensive planning; and it was held up in 1933 as an alternative to the far more complex (and as some saw it, unwieldy) NRA.

Beyond this, monetary crankiness, for example, could be seen as part of an age-old and entrenched American tradition, the tendency not to find something wrong with the "system" per se, but rather with alien intrusions into that system, be they private control of money and credit, the "crimes" of '73 or 1920, monopoly, or some other evil phenomena or individuals. Even the New Dealers' concept of limited planning could be seen as an antiplanning device in that it was advanced as an alternative to a truly planned economy. The New Dealers continually experimented with all sorts of measures—spending, monetary manipulation, NRA codes, reciprocal trade agreements —that evaded the approach to direct, detailed planning or public ownership of major industries. This was one ideological characteristic that all these groups, from New Dealers on the left to Hoover Republicans on the right, shared in common: an antipathy for central planning or public ownership, a quest for alternative programs. It was a characteristic that flowed from the antiplanning syndrome operative at the core of American ideology.

The concept of artificial prosperity entered into various analyses. Democrats of all persuasions, for example, joined in the assertion that the Republican prosperity of the twenties had been "artificial," resting on foreign loans to finance exports, and bound to come tumbling down, as it did in 1929. Conservatives of both parties insisted that the New Deal recovery of mid-decade was "artificial," sustained by federal spending, and bound to collapse when the spending slackened, as it did in 1937. Conservatives, moreover, really considered planning, like pump priming, to be a kind of artificial device, and indeed considered New Deal measures generally to be artificial; proceeding from the assumption that there was a "natural" system all departures from that system could be deemed synthetic. Critics of the New Deal, from both left and right, charged that the recovery induced by its scarcity economics, restricting production to raise prices, was contrived and artificial. Radicals could characterize the New Deal as one great artificial effort to prop a dying economic system.

Public spending could be viewed as an "artificial" device by both its friends and foes in that it was generally regarded as an emergency prop rather than as an institutionalized cure, as an external stimulus rather than as a structured part of an integrated economic system. (The fact that this "emergency" and "artificial" program of 1933 ended up by 1938 as more nearly *the* New Deal program than any other—however much it was still rationalized as an emergency device—provides a clue both as to the course of the debate, 1933–38, and to the nature of American political thinking.) Spending, in terms of its ultimate course, might even be seen as a kind of substitute for the systematic redistribution of income called for in the purchasing power thesis. Indeed, all sorts of measures—pump priming, foreign loans to finance exports, production restriction programs —could be seen as "artificial" alternatives to the institutionalization of that thesis.

Proponents of the mature economy theme could characterize any such externally induced prosperity as artificial measured against the vigor of capitalism in its expansionist phase. This thesis, held by various New Dealers, progressives, and radicals during the long depression of the thirties, has been out of vogue since World War II. Yet it is not clear that the postwar boom flowed from a renewed and dynamic capitalism rather than from the external stimulus provided by huge arms spending. Indeed, a case could be made for the proposition that the United States has not had "normal" prosperity in over a half-century—that only World War I prevented the dip of 1913–14 from turning into a protracted depression, that the prosperity of the twenties flourished through foreign loans to finance exports and analogous devices to promote domestic consumption, and that since 1940 military spending and newer equivalents of the loans of the twenties have sustained the economy.

The concepts of artificial prosperity—foreign loans, public spending, and war—were thus related to the mature economy thesis and to the depression's finale circa 1940. The mature economy theme, in all its implications, like the purchasing power thesis, was never really resolved institutionally—unless the combination of Keynesianism and war spending since 1940 may be considered such a resolution rather than, to use some favorite words of the thirties, a "palliative," an "artificial" device to bring an "artificial" prosperity, an "emergency" expedient for a multidecade "emergency." In some particulars the adherents of the mature economy theme were clearly wrong—on population, for example; on others, the Second World War undid their assumptions —economic nationalism was a wartime casualty; but their central thesis—that the historic dynamic of capitalism had given out, that intensive expansion would now have to replace extensive expansion, that the alternative to this was an economy artificially propped—remains in the limbo of theses neither proven nor disproven.

The debate ended in 1938–39 in confusion and uncertainty; no one had been proven right or wrong. The coming of World War II, of course, changed the emphasis in national discourse; foreign policy grew in importance. During the war the specter of the depression hovered in the background, and the reconversion debate included a good deal of discussion about how to meet the generally expected economic crisis. But with the failure of that crisis to materialize, and with the onset of the cold war, concern over the fundamental soundness of the economy receded into the background. None of the basic recovery formulae of the thirties had been truly implemented. The ultimate "solution," ironically, lay in a program usually advanced as a merely temporary expedient: public spending (in post-1940 military form). The debate, and, one could argue decades later, the nation's fundamental economic problem, remained unresolved.

The question of pragmatism did not inhere in the issues of planning and "systems" alone, though the rigidity of American politicians as thinkers was abundantly evident in those areas. There was a general reluctance among political leaders to confront the depression and its problems apart from preconceptions which may also have been largely misconceptions. This helps to explain not only the obvious dogmatism that was evident but also the continuing appearance and reappearance of the more subtle concepts of artificial prosperity, antiplanning, and the emergency rationale. When the realities of the depression conflicted with the ideologies of tradition, the tendency often was to stress the validity of tradition and ideology (especially among conservatives), or to grant only that ideology had to be stretched temporarily because certain expedients (such as pump priming or crop control) were necessary due to the "emergency," expedients which could be discarded upon the return of "normal" conditions (this was especially true among the more "flexible" New Dealers).

The shifting or qualified or uncertain support that characterized so many of the supporters of such programs as crop control, NRA, and pump priming showed perhaps that while men were quite aware of the malady, they were yet reluctant to stretch too much the bounds of traditional ideology in order to meet it. Such programs therefore were often presented as admittedly "artificial" and "emergency" ones. These emergency and artificial labels were perhaps indicative of the failure of American political leaders to search for and implement "permanent" remedies rather than artificial and emergency expedients—be these expedients foreign loans, pump priming, or war. There was, then, a continuing tension between emergency expedients and permanent solutions. To what extent, one may ask, did emergency expedients replace the quest for permanent programs? To what extent did they become an excuse for not confronting more basically the nation's problems? To what extent did they serve the purpose of keeping solutions within the bounds of traditional American ideology? To what extent did they provide a palliative to be used until the problem withered away?

All this was further evidence of the extraordinary persistence of traditional beliefs in American political ideology, and of the rigidity of American political leaders as thinkers. All the forces of reality—a seemingly interminable depression, millions of unemployed, poverty in the midst of plenty—could at most only shake the sacred principles, the eternal verities; certain things were forbidden and remained forbidden. This extraordinary persistence was evidenced not only by the conservatives' rigidity across the boards (as with the confidence thesis and all its applications), not only by the continuance and even revival by 1937–38 of progressive antimonopolism, not only by the dogmatism of those on the far left, not only by the New Dealers' reluctance to do anything more than bend the framework of traditional ideology, but also by positions taken on a whole range of issues—the ancient dogmas of the tariff, the reluctance to plan or to spend, the popularity of age-old monetary remedies, the unchanging horror at deviations from the true "American way."

The whole return of New Dealers by 1937–38 to some of the ancient progressive verities further showed the strength of tradition in American political thinking. Having left the epochal mood of 1933 (insofar as they, as distinct from a good part of the intellectual community, had partaken of it), New Dealers returned to the basic concepts and traditions they had known before—those of the progressive heritage; somewhat modified perhaps, more sophisticated perhaps, advanced in the name of a Gardiner Means rather than a William Jennings Bryan perhaps, but still a return to the ancient verities. The use of the term "private socialism" to describe monopoly, moreover, showed both the enduring strength of traditional concepts and the abstract quality of these concepts: "monopoly" remained the ogre, and "socialism"—of all things, the radicals' alternative to "monopoly capitalism"—was in this schema intermeshed with it.

The country seemed to some in 1933–34 to be breaking through the crust of its ideological mold, but in the end it failed to do so. The New Dealers opted for their dogmatically limited "middle way" instead, their particular path between orthodox capitalism (with its general body of theory) and orthodox socialism (with its general body of theory). Standing on middle ground, the New Dealers lacked an inclusive overall philosophy, but they clearly had operative ideological assumptions—assumptions which manifested themselves in the New Deal's NRA and AAA, which as middle way devices, deviating from all norms (left and right), were subjected to a barrage of criticism on all sides. The New Deal's purchasing power thesis, its hybrid middle way nature, its analyses but failure to develop those analyses in terms of their full implications, its bending but not breaking of traditional ideology—all these help to explain why the right could see the

New Deal as a radical phenomenon, and the far left could see it as a conservative one. The right based its analysis on the implications of the New Dealers' economic maturity and purchasing power theses, on the divergences between these theses and the conservatives' natural recovery assumptions, on the degree to which New Dealers did bend; the far left based its analysis upon the failure of the New Dealers to realize those implications and to institutionalize those theses and to transcend traditional ideology.

The New Dealers were more flexible than some. They were willing to accept "artificial" devices as long as they were recognized as artificial; they were willing to accept "temporary" expedients as long as they were recognized as temporary; they were willing to bend traditional dogmas to reach their positions as proponents of the purchasing power thesis and limited planning. But they were unwilling or unable to break free from traditional ideological restraints, to consider not only planning but central planning, not only a TVA but public ownership of key industries, not only limited devices to remix the distribution of income but more thoroughgoing devices. The New Dealers would move part way, but they would never develop—perhaps never clearly perceive—the implications of their "emergency" and "artificial" expedients. The New Dealers were the explorers of the thirties, but they broke relatively little new ground; they were pioneers, but they were relatively timid pioneers; they were humanitarians, but they failed adequately to institutionalize their humanitarianism; they were practical, but they were not pragmatic; they were experimentalists, but only within narrow bounds.

The New Dealers were merely rigid in a more flexible way. While conservatives refused even to bend traditional ideology, New Dealers bent but were unable to transcend it. All down the line—advancing the mature economy theme but never really implementing its implications, espousing the purchasing power thesis but never really institutionalizing it, rationalizing spending in terms of emergency "pump priming," pointing to the home market but opting for reciprocity, rationalizing crop control as an expedient pending the return of normal conditions, calling vaguely for "planning" but never really adopting the concept fully or meaningfully, advancing an NRA but justifying it in the name of "fair" competition, denouncing (like the conservatives) schemes more radical than their own as contrary to the American way—they moved toward a new ethos but drew back without realizing its full implications. They went a long way toward proving the validity of a pre-New Deal comment on the nature of American liberalism: "What was the 'technique of liberal failure'? It was, so Mr. Stearns said, the unwillingness of the liberal to continue with analysis once the process of analysis had become uncomfortable."[1]

The New Dealers' approach—bending but not transcending ideological norms—was what lay in part behind the conservative (and radical) charges of New Deal inconsistency. The New Dealers experimented with domestic alternatives, but legislated reciprocity; hence the charge of inconsistency. They created a National Recovery Administration, but left it too much in the hands of business; hence the charge of inconsistency. They talked about planning, but provided no central plan to coordinate the seemingly conflicting sector plans; hence the charge of inconsistency. They articulated the purchasing power thesis, but failed to institutionalize it as thoroughly as many of its advocates considered essential. They called for a pragmatic approach to problems, but failed to apply the pragmatic test to many of their own dogmatically held assumptions. They talked of the need for planning in agriculture, but rationalized crop control as a mere emergency expedient. And so on.

Moreover, Franklin Roosevelt was not sui generis; he was a reflection of the New Deal ideological type; he was an example of that type on a whole range of issues—foreign economic policy, spending, NRA, planning—albeit an example par excellence. Scholars in discussing Roosevelt's "limitations"—his reluctance to move more definitely toward Keynesianism, his inability to think critically about alternatives more radical than his own, his inability to operate outside of an existing ideological framework —have not indicated the degree to which Roosevelt's limitations were not so much peculiar to his personality, temperament, and intellectual bent as they were reflective of the limitations generally characteristic of New Dealers and progressives. *As a group* they were reluctant to move beyond pump priming as an emergency expedient; as a group they were unable to contemplate alternatives more radical than their own; as a group they were unable to operate outside of an existing ideological framework. As a group they rejected more drastic alternatives in much the same terms—vague and abstract—as those in which conservatives rejected their own reformist programs.

The phrase "middle way" was often heard during the thirties —*Sweden: The Middle Way* ran the title of a popular mid-decade book by Marquis Childs. Many defined the New Deal as a "middle way" avoiding the extremes of both laissez-faire and statism, fascism and communism. And there was merit in this view. Yet the middle way was a vast expanse; there were many middle ways. Herbert Hoover viewed his American system as a middle way between laissez-faire and economic regimentation. Norman Thomas could argue for democratic socialism as a middle way between capitalism and communism. Of the vast American middle way the New Deal preempted (and, for that matter, explored) only a relatively small part. To the left of the New Deal, the position of a native American radical such as Floyd Olson could be as fully justified in terms of the middle way rationale as that of Franklin Roosevelt. The term "regimentation" was also a distinctly relative one. Men such as James Beck and John W. Davis thought that President Hoover had set the nation upon the road to statism. Hoover denounced the New Deal in similar terms. And New Dealers declared that proposals more radical than their own threatened regimentation.

The New Deal was able and willing to disassociate liberalism from its philosophically quasi-laissez-faire economic base, from the economic liberalism of a Douglas, Mills, or Hoover; but its departure went only part way. A liberal such as John Dewey, for example, went beyond the New Deal to call for public ownership as an element of economic planning. Wrote Dewey in 1935, "The idea that liberalism cannot maintain its ends and at the same time reverse its conception of the means by which they are to be attained is folly." "The notion that organized social control of economic forces lies outside the historic path of liberalism shows that liberalism is still impeded by remnants of its earlier *laissez faire* phase. . . ."[2] On specific issues, New Dealers did use the pragmatic test to support public ownership. What was the philosophy behind TVA? ". . . it's neither fish nor fowl," said Franklin Roosevelt, "but, whatever it is, it will taste awfully good to the people of the Tennessee Valley."[3] But neither Roosevelt nor other New Dealers applied this pragmatic test to the economy as a whole; public ownership of key industries, for example, developed in terms of the American idiom, and justified in terms of public service, was apparently never even seriously considered by the administration.

Critics of the New Deal from both left and right tended to be doctrinaire in their analyses; they thought in terms of economic "systems"; they adhered to the "either-or" concept; they asserted that the New Deal *had* to fail. But New Dealers and progressives, too, did not wholly escape from this dogmatic mode of thinking; they also rejected or ignored programs (such as central planning and public ownership) on the very ground—explicit or implicit—that they were integral parts of a different or "socialist system" and were therefore inapplicable to and unadaptable by the existing or "capitalist system." Had they followed through on the pragmatic approach, had they followed through on their own basic values and analyses, they would have judged and conceivably have utilized such alternative programs *as* specific programs and on the grounds of their merits as such. But these were programs with which they would not experiment, which they would not even consider, and which, therefore, they could neither accept nor reject according to the pragmatic test. Thus, if the positions of radicals of the thirties were made rigid by dogmatic infusions of Marxism, the positions of New Dealers and progressives remained relatively rigid due to failure to transcend the doctrinaire bounds of traditional American ideology.

The New Dealers proved unable in the end to create a new reform credo to challenge the folklore of capitalism—in part, perhaps, because so many of them partook so often of the latter. No new set of attitudes emerged to challenge those shaken by the depression. Innovations in policy were, to be sure, important. The existing ethos was at least mildly modified. But there was insufficient effort to promote an overall process of ideological re-evaluation and change, a process which dovetailed with Franklin Roosevelt's educative concept of the presidency as a position of moral leadership. Such a process conceivably could have utilized America's democratic political tradition to do battle with an economic tradition called into question by the depression. It conceivably could have molded a credo out of such ongoing and accepted traditions as egalitarianism, pragmatism, and humanitarianism, fused it to political democracy, and presented it in terms of the American idiom. The New Dealers' failure to develop such a credo, their failure to transcend the folklore of capitalism, their failure to institutionalize their analyses, made it virtually impossible, once the emergency had receded, to build upon or to move beyond their New Deal.

NOTES

PROLOGUE

1 Chester Bowles *et al.*, [...] *nittee on Economic Stability* *Sponsored by Americans* [...] *n* (Washington, 1947), 5.

2 Seymour E. Harris, re [...] *s's Ordeal by Planning, The* *Journal of Business of the* [...] *go,* **XXII** (Jan. 1949), 62.

3 Rexford G. Tugwell, *A* [...] *dy* (Chicago, 1955), 326.

4 Joan Robinson, *Freedo* [...] New York: Vintage Books, 1971), 85-86.

5 John Kenneth Galbraith, [...] *nocrats and What It Takes* *to Be Needed* (New York, 1 [...]

6 Daniel R. Fusfeld, "Post- [...] attered Synthesis," *Satur-* *day Review,* **LV** (Jan. 22, 197 [...]

CHAPTER 1: THE RECOVER

1 Raymond Wolters, *Negroes* [...] *ession: The Problem of* *Economic Recovery* (Westport, ([...]

2 Schlesinger's post-1945 writin [...] voluminous. The most systematic and best-known expre [...] *Center* (Boston, 1962 [orig. pub. 1949]).

3 See esp. *The Age of Roosevelt:* [...] *eaval* (Boston, 1960), 645-57.

4 Howard Zinn, "Introduction," i [...] *New Deal Thought* (Indianapolis, 1966), esp. xxiii-iv, [...] ernstein, "The New Deal: The Conservative Achievem [...] orm," in Barton J. Bernstein, ed., *Towards a New Past:* [...] *American History* (New York, 1968), echoes Zinn.

5 Paul K. Conkin, *The New Deal* [...] , ch. 1. See also Frank A. Warren's insightful article, [...] 930's: Towards a New Perspective," in Daniel Walden, e [...] *: The Ambiguous* *Legacy* (Yellow Springs, Ohio, 1967 [...] by the present author are also relevant to this question [...] leas of Henry A.

Wallace, 1933-1948," *Agricultural History,* XLI (Apr. 1967); " 'Young Bob' La Follette on American Capitalism," *Wisconsin Magazine of History,* LV (Winter 1971-72).

6 Quoted in George H. Mayer, *The Political Career of Floyd B. Olson* (Minneapolis, 1951), 108.

CHAPTER 2: ROOTS OF THE DEBATE

1 Theodore Rosenof, " 'Young Bob' La Follette on American Capitalism," *Wisconsin Magazine of History,* LV (Winter 1971-72), 133-34; *Congressional Record (CR),* May 4, 1934, 8051-52; Frank Murphy, *Selected Addresses of Frank Murphy, Governor of Michigan, January 1, 1937, to September 30, 1938* (Lansing, 1938), 4, 98; *CR,* Apr. 13, 1936, 5423, and Dec. 14, 1937, Appendix (A) 455.

2 *CR,* Jan. 5, 1938, A 19, and Apr. 21, 1936, 5764.

3 *New York Times (NYT),* Jan. 22, 1934, 3.

4 *CR,* July 28, 1937, 7745.

5 *CR,* June 16, 1938, A 2855.

6 Testimony of Daniel W. Hoan, "Additional Public Works Appropriations," Hearing before a Subcommittee of the Committee on Education and Labor, Sen., 73d Cong., 2d Sess., May 1934, 174.

7 Norman Thomas, *The Choice before Us* (New York, 1934), 13-14, 17-18, 22-23, 28, 162; Norman Thomas, *Human Exploitation in the United States* (New York, 1934), 200-202; Norman Thomas, *After the New Deal, What?* (New York, 1936), 66, 86; Norman Thomas, *Socialism on the Defensive* (New York, 1938), 259-60; Norman Thomas, "Is Decline of the Profit Motive Desirable?" *The Rotarian,* LIII (July 1938), 9.

8 Thomas R. Amlie, "The End of Capitalism," *Common Sense,* II (Oct. 1933), 6; Thomas R. Amlie, "The Independent Farmer," *Common Sense,* IV (Sept. 1935), 18; *The Progressive,* Dec. 25, 1937, 7, and May 14, 1938, 7; Thomas R. Amlie, *The Forgotten Man's Handbook* (Elkhorn, Wis., 1936), 64-65, 67-68, 78; *CR,* Aug. 26, 1935, 14806-7.

9 Philip F. La Follette, "Reactionaries Would Starve U.S. — Phil," *The Progressive,* Sept. 15, 1934, 2.

10 Henry T. Rainey, "Our Country's Economic Strength and How to Preserve It," *The Consensus,* XVIII (Jan. 1934), 5.

11 Others expressing this idea included North Dakota Congressman Usher Burdick, Minnesota Farmer-Laborites Elmer Benson, Ernest Lundeen, and Henry Teigan, and New Dealers Kent Keller, James Murray, Homer Bone, and Josh Lee.

12 *CR,* Jan. 22, 1936, 832. Fiorello La Guardia, Harold Ickes, and Earl Browder also expressed this idea.

13 *The Progressive,* May 22, 1937, 7.

14 Theodore Rosenof, "The Economic Ideas of Henry A. Wallace, 1933-1948," *Agricultural History,* XLI (Apr. 1967), 145; Harold L. Ickes, "The Social Implications of the Roosevelt Administration," *Survey Graphic,* XXIII (Mar. 1934), 113; Harold L. Ickes, *The New Democracy* (New York, 1934), 60; Franklin D. Roosevelt, *The Public Papers and Addresses of Franklin D. Roosevelt (Public Papers),* Samuel I. Rosenman, comp. (New York, 1938-50): II, 122; III, 193-94; IV, 338.

15 Rosenof, "La Follette on American Capitalism," *Wisconsin Magazine of History,* 133-34.

16 Philip F. La Follette, "The Party of Our Time," *Vital Speeches,* IV (May 15, 1938), 451; Philip F. La Follette, "Capital on Strike," *Common Sense,* III (July 1934), 8; Philip F. La Follette, "Phil Blames Reactionaries of Both Old Parties for Bringing on Depression," *The Progressive,* July 7,

1934, 2; *NYT*, Apr. 28, 1938, 4, and June 5, 1938, 41; *The Progressive,* Jan. 9, 1937, 5, and Nov. 19, 1938, 2.

17 *CR:* Apr. 18, 1933, 1876-77; June 3, 1936, 8809-10; Feb. 6, 1936, 1603-4; June 3, 1936, 8889-90; Jan. 11, 1938, A 139; Mar. 4, 1938, A 865; June 5, 1936, 9056.

18 Roosevelt, *Public Papers,* II, 163; Lester G. Seligman and Elmer E. Cornwell, Jr., eds., *New Deal Mosaic: Roosevelt Confers with His National Emergency Council, 1933-1936* (Eugene, Ore.. 1965) 323; Franklin D. Roosevelt Press Conferences (PC): Oct. 18, 1933, 4-5, 7, 11; Dec. 29, 1933, 4; Oct. 17, 1934, 4-7; Jan. 5, 1935, 18-19. (Consulted on microfilm supplied by the Roosevelt Library.)

19 Others charging the New Deal with defeatism included Congressman Charles Halleck, and Senators Thomas Gore, James J. Davis, and Hamilton Kean.

20 Ogden L. Mills, *Liberalism Fights On* (New York, 1936), 157.

21 *CR,* June 3, 1936, 8804.

22 Alfred M. Landon, *America at the Crossroads,* Richard B. Fowler, ed. (New York, 1936), 13-15; *NYT,* May 19, 1936, 13, and June 9, 1936, 14; Donald R. McCoy, *Landon of Kansas* (Lincoln, Neb., 1966), 302.

23 Lewis W. Douglas, *The Liberal Tradition* (New York, 1935), 16, 19-22, 23 note 1; Lewis W. Douglas, "Recovery by Balanced Budget," *Review of Reviews,* XCI (Apr. 1935), 25; Lewis W. Douglas, "A Federal Fiscal Policy Conducive to Recovery," *The Consensus,* XIX (Jan. 1935), 11-12; Lewis W. Douglas, "There Is One Way Out," *The Atlantic Monthly,* CLVI (Sept. 1935), 271-72. Ogden Mills and Herbert Hoover also rejected the "overbuilt" idea.

24 *CR,* May 31, 1934, 10092-93, 10097.

25 Quoted in Herbert Hoover, *The Memoirs of Herbert Hoover: The Great Depression, 1929-1941* (New York, 1952), 252.

26 Herbert Hoover, *Addresses upon the American Road 1933-1938* (New York, 1938), 140, 179; Herbert Hoover, *America's Way Forward* (New York, n.d. [a collection of 1938-39 speeches]), 27; Herbert Hoover, *The Challenge to Liberty* (New York, 1935), 147-49.

27 Others expressing this idea included Senators Styles Bridges, Frederick Hale, and Roscoe Patterson, as well as conservative Democrats Alfred E. Smith and Newton Baker.

28 Hoover, *Challenge to Liberty,* 13, 48, 168-69; *CR,* Feb. 5, 1935, 1474; Joseph B. Ely, "Are We Worthy?" *The Saturday Evening Post,* CCIX (July 4, 1936), 72.

29 At times rather vague as to the process by which the war led to the depression, those expressing this view included Hoover, Austin, Snell, Bridges, Gore, Roscoe Patterson, David Reed, Frank Lowden, and Arthur Robinson.

30 Ogden L. Mills, *What of Tomorrow?* (New York, 1935), 3, 39, 70; Ogden L. Mills, *The Seventeen Million* (New York, 1937), 5-6, 10, 17. 88; Mills, *Liberalism Fights On,* 56-59, 64, 104, 117; Ogden L. Mills, "The American System," *Vital Speeches,* I (Aug. 26, 1935), 769.

31 Frank O. Lowden, "Can We Afford to Scrap the Constitution?" *Plain Talk Magazine,* XI (Oct. 1935), 33.

32 *CR,* May 30, 1933, 4592, and May 23, 1933, 4028; Josiah W. Bailey, "Essentials for Permanent Recovery," *Proceedings of the Academy of Political Science,* XVIII (May 1938), 47.

33 Hoover, *Challenge to Liberty,* 170; Hoover, *Addresses,* 89-90, 143-44, 203; Hoover, *America's Way Forward,* 16-17, 38.

34 Others included Austin, Patterson, Treadway, Bridges, John D. M. Hamilton, Senator Thomas Schali, and Congressmen John Taber and Charles Eaton.

35 *NYT,* Oct. 29, 1936, 12.

36 *CR,* May 21, 1934, 9128.

37 David A. Reed, "Sober Second Thought," *Vital Speeches,* I (June 17, 1935), 606.

38 *CR:* June 15, 1934, 11873-75; May 13, 1935, 7399; July 29, 1935, 12029; June 7, 1935, 8878.

39 Others advancing this argument included Treadway, Steiwer, Fish, Al Smith, Robert A. Taft, and James Wadsworth.

40 Arthur H. Vandenberg, "The Republican Indictment," *Fortune,* XIV (Oct. 1936), 183; *CR,* Feb. 13, 1936, 1954.

41 Landon, *America at the Crossroads,* 19; *NYT,* Mar. 25, 1936, 2; *CR,* Feb. 14, 1935, 1932-33; Hoover, *Challenge to Liberty,* 171; Hoover, *America's Way Forward,* 46-47; *CR,* Apr. 18, 1934, 6869, and Apr. 6, 1933, 1328. Others charging that the New Deal retarded recovery included Hamilton, Bridges, Treadway, Hatfield, and Fess.

42 Jackson speech of Jan. 6, 1938 cited in Testimony of Robert H. Jackson, "Nomination of Robert H. Jackson," Hearings before a Subcommittee of the Committee on the Judiciary, Sen., 75th Cong., 3d Sess., Feb. 1938, 109.

43 Testimony of Harry L. Hopkins, "Unemployment and Relief," Hearings before a Special Committee to Investigate Unemployment and Relief. Sen., 75th Cong., 3d Sess., Apr. 1938, 1354-55; Testimony of Harry L. Hopkins, "Emergency Relief Appropriation Act of 1938," Hearings before the Subcommittee of the Committee on Appropriations. House of Reps., 75th Cong., 3d Sess., Apr. 1938, 65-66; *CR,* June 14, 1937, A 1449.

44 *The Progressive,* May 14, 1938, 7.

45 *CR,* June 14, 1937, A 1448.

46 Among them were Senator Burton Wheeler, George Earle, and Congressmen Jerry Voorhis and Kent Keller.

47 *CR,* June 2, 1937, 5256-57, and Aug. 21, 1937, A 2369.

48 *CR,* May 10, 1938, 6588.

49 *CR,* June 16, 1938, 9684.

50 Harold L. Ickes, "Ickes Scorches Tribune, Other Reactionary Chicago Newspapers, in Campaign Talk," *The Progressive,* Oct. 31, 1936, 5.

51 *CR,* June 2, 1937, 5257.

CHAPTER 3: DEPRESSION ANALYSES

1 *Congressional Record (CR),* Apr. 25, 1933, 2312.

2 *CR,* Dec. 15, 1937, 1538.

3 Quoted in Norman Beasley, *Frank Knox, American* (New York, 1936), 155.

4 *CR,* Dec. 20, 1937, 1937.

5 Other Republican proponents of the thesis included Steiwar, Dickinson, Fish, Beck, Austin, Fess, Lowden, Patterson, Taber, Treadway, Hatfield, John D. M. Hamilton, Frederick Hale, Hamilton Kean, Everett Dirksen, Robert A. Taft, James J. Davis, Henry Fletcher, Thomas Schall, Styles Bridges, Robert Bacon, Frank Crowther, and Daniel Reed.

6 Other Democratic proponents of the thesis included Joseph Ely, Bainbridge Colby, former Maryland Governor Albert Ritchie, former Missouri Senator James Reed, Al Smith, Congressman Louis Ludlow, and Senators Edward Burke, Alva Adams, and Thomas Gore.

7 *CR,* Nov. 17, 1937, 98.

8 Ogden L. Mills, *Liberalism Fights On* (New York, 1936), 61-63.

9 *CR*, Nov. 17, 1937, 80-81, and Dec. 20, 1937, 1939; Frank Knox, *"We Planned It That Way"* (New York, 1938), 46; *CR*, Apr. 1, 1937, 3037.

10 *CR*, Dec. 13, 1937, 1401.

11 *CR*, Dec. 14, 1937, 1474.

12 *CR*, June 13, 1938, Appendix (A) 2609.

13 Norman Thomas, "Reflections on the New Depression," *Socialist Review*, VI (Jan.-Feb. 1938), 2; Norman Thomas, *Socialism on the Defensive* (New York, 1938), 260-61.

14 *CR*, Jan. 27, 1938, A 361.

15 *CR*, June 8, 1934, 10802.

16 *CR*, May 23, 1938, 7247.

17 *CR*, June 15, 1938, A 3128, and May 9, 1938, A 1883; Lewis B. Schwellenbach, "Depression or Recession," *Vital Speeches*, IV (May 15, 1938), 466; *CR*, Jan. 21, 1938, A 271.

18 Philip F. La Follette, "Capital on Strike," *Common Sense*, III (July 1934), 8. Other New Deal-progressive critics of the confidence thesis included Ickes, Earle, George Norris, Homer Bone, Josh Lee, Sherman Minton, Kent Keller, and Robert G. Allen.

19 *New York Times (NYT)*, Sept. 13, 1937, 2; Testimony of Harry L. Hopkins, "Unemployment and Relief," Hearings before a Special Committee to Investigate Unemployment and Relief, Sen., 75th Cong., 3d Sess., Apr. 1938, 1338.

20 Theodore Rosenof, "The Economic Ideas of Henry A. Wallace, 1933-1948," *Agricultural History*, XLI (Apr. 1967), 147-48; Henry A. Wallace, "The Next Four Years in Agriculture," *The New Republic*, LXXXIX (Dec. 2, 1936), 136.

21 Quoted in J. Woodford Howard, Jr., *Mr. Justice Murphy* (Princeton, 1968), 40.

22 Philip F. La Follette, "Phil Blames Reactionaries of Both Old Parties for Bringing on Depression," *The Progressive*, July 7, 1934, 2.

23 *CR*, May 15, 1935, 7567.

24 *CR*, 1933-38, *passim;* Testimony of Robert F. Wagner, "Unemployment Insurance," Hearings before a Subcommittee of the Committee on Ways and Means, House of Reps., 73d Cong., 2d Sess., Mar. 1934, 30; Testimony of Robert F. Wagner, "United States Housing Act of 1936," Hearings before the Committee on Education and Labor, Sen., 74th Cong., 2d Sess., Apr. 1936, 13-14; Testimony of Robert F. Wagner, "To Create a National Labor Board," Hearings before the Committee on Education and Labor, Sen., 73d Cong., 2d Sess., Mar. 1934, 8; Robert F. Wagner, "The Fight Has Only Begun," *American Magazine*, CXVI (Nov. 1933), 15, 84; Robert F. Wagner, "Toward Security," *The Forum and Century*, LXXXXIII (May 1935), 294-95; Robert F. Wagner, "From Drift to Mastery," *Vital Speeches*, I (Jan. 14, 1935), 247-48; Robert F. Wagner, "Primary Economic Objectives of the N.R.A.," *American Federationist*, XL (Nov. 1933), 1198-99; *NYT*: Dec. 21, 1934, 3; Jan. 20, 1936, 10; May 9, 1937, VIII, 9; Feb. 16, 1936, VII, 1; J. Joseph Huthmacher, *Senator Robert F. Wagner and the Rise of Urban Liberalism* (New York, 1968), 57-63, 156-58, 194-95.

25 Franklin D. Roosevelt, *The Public Papers and Addresses of Franklin D. Roosevelt (Public Papers)*, Samuel I. Rosenman, comp. (New York, 1938-50), III, 127.

26 Roosevelt, *Public Papers:* II, 297-98; IV, 324; V, 4, 129, 161-64, 181-82, 336, 350, 503-4; VI, 496; VII, 5, 7, 63-64, 222-23, 245; Franklin D. Roosevelt, Press Conferences (PC): July 7, 1933, 3-4; Apr. 12, 1935, 5; Oct. 30, 1935, 8; Feb. 14, 1936, 9-10; Apr. 2, 1937, 5; June 15, 1937, 7-9; Oct. 29, 1937, 3; Mar. 4, 1938, 8; Lester G. Seligman and Elmer E. Corn-

well, Jr., eds., *New Deal Mosaic: Roosevelt Confers with His National Emergency Council, 1933-1936* (Eugene, Ore., 1965), 468.

27 Norman Thomas, *Human Exploitation in the United States* (New York, 1934), 200, 379-80; Norman Thomas, *Socialism on the Defensive* (New York, 1938), 264; Norman Thomas, *The Choice before Us* (New York, 1934), 104, 218-19.

28 Norman Thomas, *A Socialist Looks at the New Deal* (n.p., [1933]), 13.

29 *NYT:* Feb. 3, 1936, 6; Sept. 7, 1936, 7; Nov. 2, 1936, 10; Norman Thomas, *The New Deal: A Socialist Analysis* (Chicago, 1933), 12; Norman Thomas, "Timely Topics," *The New Leader,* Apr. 28, 1934, sect. 2, 8; Thomas, *Human Exploitation,* 384; Norman Thomas, *After the New Deal, What?* (New York, 1936), 25; Norman Thomas, *Shall Labor Support Roosevelt?* (n.p., [a Sept. 8, 1936 speech]), 12.

30 Thomas, *Human Exploitation,* 203-4.

31 Still others who supported one point or another of the purchasing power thesis included New Dealers and progressives Schwellenbach, Pepper, James Murray, Robert G. Allen, George Norris, Gerald Nye, Alben Barkley, Homer Bone, Edward Costigan, Robert Jackson, Jerry Voorhis, Bronson Cutting, Josh Lee, Herbert Lehman, Kent Keller, Theodore Francis Green, James Pope, Gerald Boileau, David J. Lewis, and Joseph O'Mahoney, radicals and Farmer-Laborites Upton Sinclair, Ernest Lundeen, Henry Teigan, Floyd Olson, Elmer Benson, Vito Marcantonio, and Howard Y. Williams, and unorthodox Democrat Huey Long.

32 *CR,* May 4, 1934, 8053.

33 Jerry Voorhis, *Confessions of a Congressman* (Garden City, N.Y., 1947), 82.

34 *CR,* Jan. 27, 1934, 1456. Other Democratic critics included James Byrnes, Joseph Robinson, M. M. Logan, Bennett Champ Clark, John Bankhead, Pat Harrison, Tom Connally, John Rankin, Sam Rayburn, and Robert Doughton, New Dealers and progressives Roosevelt, Wagner, Wheeler, Wallace, Ickes, Alben Barkley, Edward Costigan, Otha Wearin, George McGill, and James Pope, and conservatives Carter Glass, Lewis Douglas, Newton Baker, Alva Adams, William H. King, and Thomas Gore.

35 *CR,* Feb. 19, 1935, 2191.

36 *CR,* June 4, 1934, 10360.

37 *Amend Tariff Act of 1930: Reciprocal Trade Agreements,* 73d Cong., 2d Sess., House Report No. 1000; *CR:* Mar. 23, 1934, 5256-60; May 17, 1934, 8987-88, 8992, 8994; June 11, 1934, 11006; June 15, 1934, 11839; Mar. 6, 1935, 3044, 3046-49; Jan. 23, 1936, 950; Feb. 23, 1937, 1493, 1499-500; June 16, 1938, A 2925.

38 Arthur M. Schlesinger, Jr., *The Age of Roosevelt: The Crisis of the Old Order* (Boston, 1957), 289, 428; Frank Freidel, *Franklin D. Roosevelt: The Triumph* (Boston, 1956), 268, 315, 354, 356-57, 368-69; Thomas H. Greer, *What Roosevelt Thought* (East Lansing, Mich., 1958), 59; Arhur M. Schlesinger, Jr., *The Age of Roosevelt: The Coming of the New Deal* (Boston, 1959), 192; Roosevelt, *Public Papers,* III, 115, and IV, 463-64. Others arguing that a healthy export trade was vital to domestic prosperity included Joseph Robinson, Allen Ellender, Kenneth McKellar, William Bankhead, and Samuel McReynolds, New Dealers and progressives Burt Wheeler, Maury Maverick, Byron Harlan, Alben Barkley, James Pope, and Otha Wearin, and conservatives Lewis Douglas, Millard Tydings, Walter George, and Thomas Gore.

39 Henry A. Wallace, *America Must Choose* (New York, 1934), 17 and *passim.*

40 *NYT,* Oct. 23, 1936, 19; Testimony of Lewis W. Douglas, "Extending Reciprocal Trade Agreement Act," Hearings before the Committee on Finance, Sen., 75th Cong., 1st Sess., Feb. 1937, 513-14; Lewis W. Douglas,

The Liberal Tradition (New York, 1935), vii-viii, 122; Lewis W. Douglas, "Balancing the National Budget," *The Consensus,* XXII (Jan. 1938), 17; Lewis W. Douglas, "Government Fiscal Policies," *The Bankers Magazine,* CXXXI (July 1935), 77. Others advancing this antiregimentation theme included John W. Davis, Henry Stimson, Elbert Thomas, and Congressmen Martin Dies and John Lambeth.

41 *CR,* May 30, 1934, 9985.

42 *CR,* Apr. 4, 1934, 6051, and May 23, 1934, 9394-95.

43 *CR,* Jan. 23, 1936, 951.

44 Joseph E. Reeve, *Monetary Reform Movements* (Washington, 1943), 13, 35, 38, 44, 46, 53, 57, 105, 110, 126.

45 Eric Manheimer, "The Public Career of Elmer Thomas" (Ph.D. thesis, University of Oklahoma, 1952), 9, 18; Reeve, *Monetary Reform Movements,* 96, 148-60, 261, 380; *CR,* 1934-38, *passim;* Elmer Thomas, "Money and Its Management," *Annals of the American Academy of Political and Social Science,* CLXXI (Jan. 1934), 132-33, 135; Elmer Thomas, "Tinkering with the Currency," *The Bankers Magazine,* CXXVII (Dec. 1933), 606-7; *NYT:* July 16, 1933, VIII, 2; Dec. 24, 1933, IV, 4; Nov. 8, 1934, 2.

46 *CR:* Mar. 9, 1933, 83; Mar. 22, 1933, 736-37; Mar. 27, 1933, 893; Apr. 6, 1933, 1369-70; May 2, 1933, 2714-15, 2768-69; June 10, 1933, 5663; Feb. 20, 1934, 2883-84; Apr. 16, 1934, 6671-73; Aug. 23, 1935, 14408; Mar. 3, 1936, 3152; Reeve, *Monetary Reform Movements,* 9, 36, 99-100, 191-92.

47 *CR,* May 30, 1934, 10024, and *CR,* 1933-36, 1938, *passim.*

48 Reeve, *Monetary Reform Movements,* 10, 21-22, 35, 68, 120.

49 *Ibid.,* 69, 241-42; Burton K. Wheeler with Paul F. Healy, *Yankee from the West* (Garden City, N.Y., 1962), 302.

50 Manheimer, "Elmer Thomas," 155; David Owen Powell, "The Union Party of 1936" (Ph.D. thesis, Ohio State University, 1962), 70.

51 Others urging or attracted to monetary formulae included Senators Lynn Frazier, Key Pittman, Ellison D. ("Cotton Ed") Smith, John Bankhead, and Tom Connally, and Congressmen Byron Harlan, Marvin Jones, Usher Burdick, Martin Dies, Clarence Cannon, Henry Steagall, Fred Vinson, Kent Keller, and Jerry Voorhis.

52 *CR,* Nov. 23, 1937, A 160.

53 *CR,* Dec. 3, 1937, 815.

54 *CR,* Jan. 13, 1938, A 184, and June 16, 1938, A 2950-51; *NYT,* May 11, 1938, 1, and June 19, 1938, 2; Bertrand H. Snell, "Bankruptcy and Moral Disintegration," *Vital Speeches,* IV (July 15, 1938), 596.

55 Frank Knox, *"We Planned It That Way"* (New York, 1938), 9, 47, 54, 59, 64-65; Frank Knox, "A Republican Program," *Vital Speeches,* IV (Feb. 1, 1938), 243, 246; *CR,* Apr. 15, 1938, A 1541. Others expressing the "political" recession concept included Bailey, Hoover, Landon, Taber, Austin, Treadway, Hamilton, Fish, Joe Martin, Peter Gerry, Daniel Reed, and Robert Bacon.

56 Others included James J. Davis, Everett Dirksen, Daniel Reed, Robert Bacon, and Frank Crowther.

57 *CR,* June 15, 1938, A 3128.

58 *CR,* June 16, 1938, A 2889. Tom Amlie, Claude Pepper, and Jerry Voorhis also rejected the conservatives' tax argument.

59 Roosevelt, PC, Oct. 4, 1938, 13.

60 *CR,* Mar. 24, 1938, 4050. Others advancing the concept included Alben Barkley, Claude Pepper, James Pope, Robert Jackson, and Lewis Schwellenbach.

61 *NYT,* Jan. 23, 1938, 8.

62   Roosevelt, *Public Papers,* VI, 520, and VII, xxii-xxiii.

63   Robert F. Wagner, "Pump-Priming," *Vital Speeches,* IV (June 1, 1938), 482. Others focusing on spending included Barkley, Pepper, Schwellenbach, Homer Bone, Kent Keller, James Mead, Frank Murphy, and Elmer Benson.

64   Testimony of Fiorello H. La Guardia. "Unemployment and Relief," Hearings before a Special Committee to Investigate Unemployment and Relief, Sen., 75th Cong., 3d Sess., Jan. 1938, 555.

65   *CR:* May 23, 1938, 7247-48, 7250-53, 7255; Apr. 7, 1938, A 1377; May 23, 1938, A 2087-89; May 27, 1938, A 2185; June 16, 1938, A 2873.

66   *CR:* Nov. 16, 1937, A 50; Jan. 10, 1938, A 133; Jan. 11, 1938, A 139; Mar. 8, 1938, A 1000.

67   Thomas, *Socialism on the Defensive,* 259-63; Thomas, Reflections on the New Depression," *Socialist Review,* 1-2.

68   *CR,* Jan. 5, 1938, 60.

69   *CR,* Jan. 19, 1938, 802.

70   *CR,* Jan. 18, 1938, 738, and Mar. 31, 1938, 4466.

71   Wagner, "From Drift to Mastery," *Vital Speeches,* 248; *CR,* Feb. 3, 1936, 1338.

72   Henry A. Wallace, "Agricultural Security," in Edwin G. Nourse, *et al., Three Years of the Agricultural Adjustment Administration* (Washington, 1937), 572; Testimony of Henry A. Wallace, "Emergency Relief Appropriation Act of 1937," Hearings before the Subcommittee of the Committee on Appropriations, House of Reps., 75th Cong., 1st Sess., May 1937, 7; John Morton Blum, *From the Morgenthau Diaries: Years of Crisis 1928-1938* (Boston, 1959), 385.

73   Testimony of La Guardia, "Unemployment and Relief," 557. Others reflecting this view of spending included FDR, Frank Murphy, George Earle, Harold Ickes, Burt Wheeler, George Norris, James Mead, and Byron Harlan.

74   *CR,* Jan. 15, 1936, 449.

75   L. J. Dickinson, "Agriculture and Its Future," *Vital Speeches,* II (Nov. 18, 1935), 105.

76   *CR,* Feb. 15, 1935, 2024. Others pursuing this "artificial prosperity" theme included Bailey, Hoover, Mills, Knox, Byrd, Landon, Austin, Bridges, Steiwer, Henry Fletcher, and Senators Roscoe Patterson, Royal Copeland, and W. Warren Barbour.

77   Others included Democrats Millard Tydings, Al Smith, Bainbridge Colby, John W. Davis, Eugene Talmadge, Thomas Gore, William H. King, Albert Ritchie, Joseph Ely, James Reed, and Louis Ludlow, and Republicans Vandenberg, Dickinson, Lowden, Taber, Fish, Bridges, Joe Martin, David Reed, Arthur Robinson, James Wadsworth, Henry Fletcher, Charles Halleck, and Theodore Christianson.

78   *CR,* June 16, 1937, 5809. Progressive George Norris and New Dealer Harold Ickes echoed the call for retrenchment. Others who urged a return to fiscal orthodoxy during this period, often on the ground that the crisis had passed, included Democrats Bailey, Byrd, Tydings, M. M. Logan, Alva Adams, Walter George, Pat Harrison, Joseph Robinson, Kenneth McKellar, and Robert Doughton—some of whom, as loyal party men, would have been more likely to have accepted the 1933-34 "emergency rationale" of the administration than would their GOP counterparts.

79   John D. M. Hamilton, "Issues of the Campaign: Two Views," *The Christian Science Monitor Weekly Magazine Section,* Oct. 5, 1938, 3.

80   *NYT,* Apr. 23, 1938, 1.

81   *CR:* Dec. 21, 1937, A 614; Apr. 11, 1938, A 1464; May 11, 1938, 6649-50. Others arguing that pump priming had been tried, had failed, and ought

not to be tried again, included Josiah Bailey, Arthur Vandenberg, Harry Byrd, Millard Tydings, James J. Davis, Henry Cabot Lodge, Jr., and Robert A. Taft.

82   *CR,* May 23, 1938, A 2097-98.

83   *CR,* May 23, 1938, 7245, 7255, A 2087, and June 16, 1938, A 2873.

84   *CR,* June 6, 1938, A 2373. Fiorello La Guardia, Elmer Benson, and Congressman Jerry O'Connell were also among those who supported renewed spending on an "emergency" basis, stressing that it did not provide a "permanent" solution.

CHAPTER 4: FARM POLICY

1   *Congressional Record (CR),* July 20, 1935, 11499.

2   Gerald P. Nye, "Under the Bankers' Thumb," *Common Sense,* III (March 1934), 12.

3   *CR,* March 3, 1934, 3646.

4   *CR,* Apr. 7, 1933, 1396.

5   *CR,* May 22, 1935, 8016.

6   *CR,* Dec. 3, 1937, 812.

7   *CR,* Feb. 27, 1934, 3341, and May 26, 1936, 7983.

8   *CR,* Jan. 24, 1934, 1243-44. Others placing the problem in this crop control-or-export trade expansion context included Jimmy Byrnes, John Bankhead, Henry Wallace, James Pope, Robert Doughton, George McGill, Henry Rainey, Byron Harlan, John Lambeth, Marvin Jones, and Joseph Byrns.

9   Franklin D. Roosevelt, Press Conferences (PC), Aug. 3, 1937, 4-8.

10   Franklin D. Roosevelt, *The Public Papers and Addresses of Franklin D. Roosevelt (Public Papers),* Samuel I. Rosenman, comp. (New York, 1938-50), VI, 432.

11   *CR,* Dec. 3, 1937, 811.

12   *New York Times (NYT),* Dec. 3, 1937, 10; Norman Thomas, "The Campaign of 1934," *American Socialist Quarterly,* III (Autumn 1934), 4; Upton Sinclair, *We, People of America and How We Ended Poverty* (Pasadena, 1935), 51; Upton Sinclair, *I, Candidate for Governor: And How I Got Licked* (Pasadena, 1935), 65; *CR,* Jan. 22, 1936, 882-83, and Feb. 20, 1936, 2529-31.

13   Henry A. Wallace, *New Frontiers* (New York, 1934), 139.

14   *CR,* June 28, 1937, Appendix (A) 1606, and Nov. 26, 1937, 385-86.

15   *NYT,* Nov. 6, 1934, 20.

16   Still others included Royal Copeland, Al Smith, Bertrand Snell, David Reed, Joe Martin, and Massachusetts Democratic Senator David Walsh.

17   Norman Thomas, "Starve and Prosper!" *Current History,* XL (May 1934), 137; Norman Thomas, "Timely Topics," *The New Leader,* Nov. 18, 1933, 8, and Apr. 28, 1934, sect. 2, 8; Norman Thomas, "A Party of Three Messiahs and a Presidential Candidate," *Socialist Call,* June 27, 1936, 12; Norman Thomas, "At the Front," *Socialist Call,* July 3, 1937, 4, and Dec. 18, 1937, 4; H. J. Voorhis, "Before Agriculture Can Be Planned," *The World Tomorrow,* XVII (Feb. 15, 1934), 79.

18   *CR,* Mar. 5, 1935, 2980.

19   *NYT,* Mar. 31, 1935, VII, 3.

20   *CR,* Apr. 17, 1933, 1831, and Feb. 14, 1936, 2034.

21   *CR,* Aug. 17, 1935, 13592.

22   *CR,* July 16, 1935, 11223.

23   Other farm state leaders upset about NRA's impact included William Langer, Clyde Herring, Louis Murphy, and Charles Bryan.

24   *CR*, Mar. 5, 1934, 3671.

25   *CR*, Feb. 20, 1936, 2513; *NYT*, Sept. 25, 1935, 4. Herbert Hoover, Ogden Mills, and L. J. Dickinson also argued in this vein.

26   Others included Dickinson, Fish, Byrd, and Fess.

27   *CR*, May 4, 1938, 6225.

28   Smith comment during testimony, "Agricultural Emergency Act to Increase Farm Purchasing Power," Hearings before the Committee on Agriculture and Forestry, Sen., 73d Cong., 1st Sess., Mar. 1933, 84.

29   Norman Thomas, "Timely Topics," *The New Leader*, Mar. 25, 1933, 16.

30   *NYT*, July 5, 1934, 13.

31   *NYT*, June 3, 1935, 15.

32   Edward L. and Frederick H. Schapsmeier, *Henry A. Wallace of Iowa: The Agrarian Years, 1910-1940* (Ames, Iowa, 1968), 180; Arthur M. Schlesinger, Jr., *The Age of Roosevelt: The Coming of the New Deal* (Boston, 1959), 66; Theodore Rosenof, "Henry Wallace: A New Dealer's Ideology, 1933-1948" (B.A. thesis, Rutgers University, 1965), 43.

33   Roosevelt, PC, Jan. 10, 1936, 8.

34   *CR*, Apr. 28, 1933, 2554.

35   *CR*, Mar. 27, 1934, 5503.

36   *CR*, Mar. 24, 1934, 5312.

37   Norman Thomas, "Timely Topics," *The New Leader*, Apr. 28, 1934, sect. 2, 8; Norman Thomas, *The Plight of the Share-Cropper* (New York, 1934), 16-17; Thomas, "Starve and Prosper!" *Current History*, 137.

38   Henry A. Wallace, *America Must Choose* (New York, 1934), 9.

39   *CR*, Mar. 13, 1935, 3564-65.

40   John L. Shover, "Populism in the Nineteen-Thirties: The Battle for the AAA," *Agricultural History*, XXXIX (Jan. 1965), 17, 19; Allan Seymour Everest, *Morgenthau, the New Deal, and Silver* (New York, 1950), 24, 56; Joseph E. Reeve, *Monetary Reform Movements* (Washington, 1943), 26, 30, 38, 61, 98-99, 192; William E. Leuchtenburg, *Franklin D. Roosevelt and the New Deal* (New York, 1963), 50-51; Schlesinger, *Coming of the New Deal*, 41, 236; Van L. Perkins, "The AAA and the Politics of Agriculture: Agricultural Policy Formulation in the Fall of 1933," *Agricultural History*, XXXIX (Oct. 1965), 222-23.

41   *CR*, Mar. 27, 1934, 5486-87, 5503.

42   *CR*, July 20, 1935, 11501.

43   George D. Aiken, *Speaking from Vermont* (New York, 1938), 219-20.

44   Charles McNary, "Republicanism—Its Future," *The Christian Science Monitor Weekly Magazine Section*, Apr. 27, 1938, 2. Others attracted to such schemes included Vandenberg, Snell, Joe Martin, Fish, Wheeler, Lynn Frazier, Josh Lee, Arthur Capper, Usher Burdick, Theodore Christianson, Richard Russell, Martin Dies, Walter George, and Josiah Bailey.

45   *CR:* July 18, 1935, 11394, 11396; Feb. 13, 1936, 1957-59; Feb. 14, 1936, 2041; Aug. 11, 1937, 8677; Aug. 20, 1937, 9432; Aug. 21, 1937, 9576; Tom Connally, *My Name Is Tom Connally* (New York, 1954), 162; Testimony of Tom Connally, "Include Cattle as Basic Agricultural Commodity," Hearing before the Committee on Agriculture, House of Reps., 73d Cong., 2d Sess., Jan. 1934, 42.

46   Others included Joe Martin, Warren Austin, Herbert Lehman, and Upton Sinclair.

47   *CR*, Feb. 14, 1936, 2034-35, 2037.

48   William E. Borah, "The Farmer's Enemy," *Collier's*, LXXXXVII (Feb.

1, 1936), 12-13, 44; *CR:* Jan. 18, 1934, 872-74; Feb. 8, 1934, 2157; Mar. 23, 1934, 5220; Feb. 11, 1935, 1799; July 1, 1937, 6673; May 12, 1936, 7044; Nov. 19, 1937, 166; Dec. 3, 1937, 813; Dec. 8, 1937, 1065; Feb. 14, 1938, 1882, 1885.

CHAPTER 5: ECONOMIC PLANNING

1, 1936), 12-13, 44; *CR:* Jan. 18, 1934, 872-74; Feb. 8, 1934, 2157; Mar. XXII (Aug. 1933), 395.

2 Theodore Rosenof, "The Economic Ideas of Henry A. Wallace, 1933-1948," *Agricultural History,* XLI (Apr. 1967), 145-46.

3 Franklin D. Roosevelt, *The Public Papers and Addresses of Franklin D. Roosevelt (Public Papers),* Samuel I. Rosenman, comp. (New York, 1938-50), V, 425.

4 *Congressional Record (CR),* Jan. 4, 1934, 70.

5 Other such critics included Roscoe Patterson, John Taber, Henry Fletcher, Walter George, William H. King, Thomas Gore, Bainbridge Colby, and Albert Ritchie.

6 *New York Times (NYT),* Jan. 25, 1936, 6.

7 *CR:* May 30, 1934, 9973; July 17, 1935, 11288; Feb. 21, 1935, 2383.

8 Herbert Hoover, *The Challenge to Liberty* (New York, 1935), 171.

9 *CR,* Aug. 24, 1935, 14467.

10 L. J. Dickinson, "Return to Representative Government," *Vital Speeches,* II (Dec. 16, 1935), 161-62; *CR,* June 21, 1935, 9821.

11 Ogden L. Mills, *What of Tomorrow?* (New York, 1935), 13. Vandenberg, Dickinson, King, Hoover, Douglas, Taft, and Austin also argued in this vein.

12 Those focusing on the contradictions of New Deal planning included Hoover, Steiwer, Snell, Treadway, Dirksen, Hamilton, and Congressman Clifford Hope.

13 Norman Thomas, *The New Deal: A Socialist Analysis* (Chicago, 1933), 3; Norman Thomas, "The New Deal: No Program of Security," *The Southern Review,* I (Autumn 1935), 367-68; *NYT,* Feb. 3, 1936, 6, and June 7, 1936, VII, 3; Norman Thomas, "At the Front," *Socialist Call,* Nov. 20, 1937, 4; Norman Thomas, *Human Exploitation in the United States* (New York, 1934), 204.

14 Lewis W. Douglas, *The Liberal Tradition* (New York, 1935), 56. Others proceeding in this vein included Hoover, Mills, Knox, Bailey, Lowden, Dickinson, Taft, and Theodore Christianson.

15 Hoover, *Challenge to Liberty,* 116; Ogden L. Mills, *The Seventeen Million* (New York, 1937), 27; Ogden L. Mills, *Liberalism Fights On* (New York, 1936), 82-83, 86-87, 89; Douglas, *Liberal Tradition,* 40-41, 46; Frank Knox, *"We Planned It That Way"* (New York, 1938), 54.

16 *The Progressive,* Sept. 7, 1935, 3; Thomas R. Amlie, "Essence of New Deal Lies in Artificial Scarcity: Rep. Amlie," *The Progressive,* Dec. 7, 1935, 3; Thomas R. Amlie, *The Forgotten Man's Handbook* (Elkhorn, Wis., 1936), 71, 93, 126; Thomas R. Amlie, "Maldistribution of Wealth Blocking Recovery: Amlie," *The Progressive,* Dec. 21, 1935, 5; *CR,* Aug. 26, 1935, 14802-4.

17 Norman Thomas, *A Socialist Looks at the New Deal* (n.p., [1933]), 13; Norman Thomas, "Surveying the New Deal," *The World Tomorrow,* XVII (Jan. 18, 1934), 37; Norman Thomas, "At the Front," *Socialist Call,* Aug. 13, 1938, 5; Norman Thomas, "Timely Topics," *The New Leader,* Apr. 28, 1934, sect. 2, 8; Norman Thomas, "Starve and Prosper!" *Current History,* XL (May 1934), 138.

18 Robert H. Jackson, "Financial Monopoly: The Road to Socialism,"

The Forum, C (Dec. 1938), 307; Ellis W. Hawley. *The New Deal and the Problem of Monopoly* (Princeton. 1966), 402; *NYT*. Jan. 29, 1938, 3, and Jan. 30, 1937, 6; *CR*, Jan. 31, 1938. Appendix (A) 379-80.

19 Rosenof, "Economic Ideas of Wallace," *Agricultural History*, 145-46.

20 *CR*, Jan. 31, 1938, 1266.

21 Franklin D. Roosevelt, Press Conferences (PC), Feb. 4, 1938, 4.

22 Roosevelt, *Public Papers*, II, 246.

23 *CR*, Apr. 21, 1936, 5764; *NYT*, Nov. 29, 1936, VIII, 5.

24 Frank Murphy. *Selected Addresses of Frank Murphy, Governor of Michigan, January 1, 1937, to September 30, 1938* (Lansing, Mich., 1938), 4.

25 *CR*, Jan. 30, 1936, 1278.

26 Hawley, *New Deal and Monopoly*, 29.

27 *CR*, June 13, 1933, 5837.

28 *CR:* June 7, 1933, 5152-53, 5163; June 13, 1933, 5837; May 23, 1934, 9334; Wagner, "Planning in Place of Restraint," *Survey Graphic*, 396.

29 Testimony of Robert F. Wagner, "National Industrial Recovery," Committee on Finance, Sen., 73d Cong., 1st Sess., May 1933, 2-3,6; Testimony of Robert F. Wagner, "National Industrial Recovery," Hearings before the Committee on Ways and Means. House of Reps.. 73d Cong., 1st Sess.. May 1933, 95-96; *NYT*, May 28, 1933, VIII, 3; *CR:* June 7, 1933, 5152-55, 5157-58, 5163-64; June 8, 1933, 5235-38, 5245; June 13, 1933, 5837.

30 *CR*, May 15, 1935, 7568; Robert F. Wagner, "The Fight Has Only Begun," *American Magazine*, CXVI (Nov. 1933), 84. Testimony of Robert F. Wagner, "To Create a National Labor Board," Hearings before the Committee on Education and Labor, Sen., 73d Cong., 2d Sess., Mar. 1934, 7-8; *CR*, Mar. 21, 1935, 4167; Robert F. Wagner, "From Drift to Mastery," *Vital Speeches*, I (Jan. 14, 1935), 248; *NYT*, May 9, 1937, VIII, 9.

31 *CR:* June 17, 1935, 9417-18; Aug. 23, 1935, 14230; June 14, 1938, 9173; Apr. 20, 1936, 5691.

32 Roosevelt, *Public Papers*, II, 202, 253, 255; III, 125, 129.

33 Roosevelt, PC, Dec. 29, 1933, 2; Roosevelt, *Public Papers*, III, 57, 132.

34 Roosevelt, *Public Papers:* V, 346; III, 137-38; VI, 520.

35 *CR:* Jan. 31, 1935, 1334; May 31, 1935, 8473; June 7, 1935, 8887-88; June 14, 1935, 9315-16; Feb. 25, 1937, A 337.

36 Such conservatives as Hoover, Knox, Mills, Dickinson, Tydings, Fess, Hatfield, Patterson, Thomas Schall, David Reed, and Al Smith all criticized the NRA.

37 *CR:* June 16, 1934, 12052.

38 Norman Thomas, *After the New Deal, What?* (New York, 1936), 28; Norman Thomas, *The Choice before Us* (New York, 1934), 104. 105 note 1; Thomas, *Human Exploitation*, 206-7; Norman Thomas, "Why I Am a Socialist," *Independent Woman*, XIII (Oct. 1934), 333; *NYT*, Nov. 5, 1934, 10; Norman Thomas, "Timely Topics," *The New Leader:* May 20, 1933, 12; July 1, 1933, 12; Nov. 11, 1933, 8; Feb. 10, 1934, 8; May 12. 1934, sect. 2, 12; Norman Thomas, "At the Front," *Socialist Call*, June 1, 1935, 5, and June 8, 1935, 5.

39 *CR:* June 8, 1933, 5238, and June 13, 1933, 5843-45.

40 *CR:* June 7, 1933, 5162-66; June 13, 1933, 5836-37, 5841-42; Jan. 18, 1934, 872-76; Jan. 31, 1934, 1652-53; Feb. 8, 1934, 2157-58; Mar. 21, 1934, 5000-5001; Feb. 28, 1935, 2736; Mar. 8, 1935, 3198, 3201; *NYT*, Sept. 7, 1933, 10, and Nov. 6, 1933, 8.

41 *CR:* Jan. 18, 1934, 866-71; Jan. 22, 1934, 1077-81; Jan. 27, 1934, 1442-44; May 22, 1934, 9234-36, 9240; May 23, 1934, 9321-23, 9327-28; June 16, 1934, 12050; Gerald P. Nye, "Squeezing the Consumer," *Current*

History, XL (June 1934), 291-95; Gerald P. Nye, "Under the Bankers' Thumb," *Common Sense,* III (Mar. 1934), 13.

42 *NYT,* Jan. 3, 1937, VIII, 17; Philip F. La Follette, "Useful Work, Not Doles," *The Progressive,* Feb. 8, 1936, 1; *The Progressive,* Apr. 30, 1938, 3; Philip F. La Follette, "The Party of Our Time," *Vital Speeches,* IV (May 15, 1938), 450-52.

43 Max Lerner, *Ideas for the Ice Age* (New York, 1941), 222.

44 *CR,* May 4, 1938, 6226.

45 Hawley, *New Deal and Monopoly,* 181-83; Arthur M. Schlesinger, Jr., *The Age of Roosevelt: The Politics of Upheaval* (Boston, 1960), 217.

46 *CR,* June 11, 1938, A 2585.

47 *CR:* June 23, 1937, A 1576, A 1578; Aug. 16, 1937, A 2483; May 27, 1938, 7671-72; Jerry Voorhis, "Legislating Abundance," *Common Sense,* VII (Feb. 1938), 13.

48 Voorhis, "Legislating Abundance," *Common Sense,* 13; *CR,* Aug. 16, 1937, A 2481, A 2483-84, and June 23, 1937, A 1577-78.

49 *CR,* June 23, 1937, A 1577; Voorhis, "Legislating Abundance," *Common Sense,* 14; Jerry Voorhis, "Abundance—or War?" *Common Sense,* VII (Mar. 1938), 15-16.

50 Marian C. McKenna, *Borah* (Ann Arbor, Mich., 1961), 317; *CR:* June 7, 1937, 5362-63; Feb. 14, 1938, 1884; May 28, 1938, 7473, 7475.

51 *CR:* Aug. 6, 1935, 12552, 12555; Aug. 26, 1935, 14703; Feb. 4, 1936, 1432-34; Apr. 7, 1937, 3244; Jan. 15, 1937, A 43-45; Nov. 30, 1937, 494; Nov. 23, 1937, A 162-63; Dec. 21, 1937, A 572-73; Jan. 5, 1938, A 15; Joseph C. O'Mahoney, "Federal Incorporation of Interstate Commerce," *Vital Speeches,* III (Jan. 1, 1937), 173-74; Joseph C. O'Mahoney, "The American Ideal," *Vital Speeches,* IV (Feb. 1, 1938), 247-49.

52 John P. Frank, *Mr. Justice Black* (New York, 1949), 88-89; Arthur M. Schlesinger, Jr., *The Age of Roosevelt: The Coming of the New Deal* (Boston, 1959), 91; Charles A. Madison, *Leaders and Liberals in 20th Century America* (New York, 1961), 370; *CR:* May 27, 1933, 4432; Feb. 8, 1935, 1715-16; July 28, 1937, 7746; June 15, 1937, A 1481-82; Testimony of Hugo L. Black, "Thirty-Hour Work Week," Hearings before a Subcommittee of the Committee on the Judiciary, Sen., 74th Cong., 1st Sess., Jan. 1935, 5-6, 8, 10-13; Hugo Black, "My Views on the Short Work Week," *Common Sense,* IV (Feb. 1935), 23; Hugo Black, "The Shorter Work Week and Work Day," *Annals of the American Academy of Political and Social Science,* CLXXXIV (Mar. 1936), 62, 65-66.

53 *CR,* June 20, 1936, 10745.

54 Roosevelt, *Public Papers,* VII, 311-12.

55 *NYT,* Nov. 4, 1938, 18; *CR,* June 16, 1938, A 2872.

CHAPTER 6: ECONOMIC SYSTEMS

1 *Congressional Record (CR):* May 12, 1936, 7043-44; Apr. 1, 1937, 3005; May 25, 1938, 7473; William E. Borah, "The Liberty League," *Vital Speeches,* I (Oct. 22, 1934), 64; William E. Borah, "The Farmer's Enemy," *Collier's,* LXXXXVII (Feb. 1, 1936), 13, 43-44; *New York Times (NYT),* May 29, 1936, 13.

2 *NYT,* June 17, 1937, 16, and Dec. 9, 1938, 22; *CR:* Mar. 22, 1934, 5096; June 18, 1935, 9510; Aug. 26, 1935, 14702-3; Feb. 4, 1936, 1434; Mar. 19, 1937, 2491; June 1, 1937, 5131-32; Nov. 23, 1937, Appendix (A) 162; Jan. 5, 1938, A 16-17; June 9, 1938, 8596.

3 *CR:* Feb. 6, 1935, 1525; Feb. 19, 1935, 2199-205; Mar. 28, 1935, 4607; Apr. 3, 1935, 4903; Apr. 12, 1935, 5847; June 11, 1935, 9043; June 6, 1936, 9133-34; Mar. 4, 1938, 2833.

4   Jonathan Mitchell, "Jackson Democrat," *The New Republic*, LXXXXIII (Jan. 26, 1938), 327.

5   *CR*, Mar. 4, 1938, 2833.

6   Testimony of Robert H. Jackson, "Nomination of Robert H. Jackson," Hearings before a Subcommittee of the Committee on the Judiciary, Sen., 75th Cong., 3d Sess., Feb. 1938, 28; "Robert H. Jackson," *Fortune*, XVII (Mar. 1938), 134.

7   Robert H. Jackson, "The Philosophy of Big Business," *Vital Speeches*, IV (Jan. 15, 1938), 208-10; Robert H. Jackson, "Should the Antitrust Laws Be Revised?" *United States Law Review*, LXXI (Oct. 1937), 577, 582; Testimony of Jackson, "Nomination of Robert H. Jackson," 110; *CR*, May 28, 1937, A 1293-94, and Jan. 5, 1938, A 29; *NYT*: Sept. 18, 1937, 30; Jan. 29, 1938, 3; Feb. 25, 1938, 7; Feb. 13, 1938, VIII, 4; Robert H. Jackson, "Financial Monopoly: The Road to Socialism," *The Forum*, C (Dec. 1938), 303-5, 307.

8   Jonathan Mitchell, "Borah Knows Best," *The New Republic*, LXXXV (Jan. 29, 1936), 334; Ellis W. Hawley, *The New Deal and the Problem of Monopoly* (Princeton, 1966), 295; *NYT*, Dec. 28, 1937, 6.

9   *CR:* Mar. 8, 1935, 3202; Mar. 15, 1935, 3710, 3714; Mar. 21, 1935, 4165-66; May 16, 1935, 7665-66; July 17, 1935, 11288; Apr. 29, 1936, 6347; May 12, 1936, 7043; May 29, 1936, 8286; Mar. 19, 1937, 2477-78, 2494; Apr. 5, 1937, 3137-38; June 7, 1937, 5362-63; Dec. 3, 1937, 812; Feb. 14, 1938, 1882-85; May 25, 1938, 7471-72, 7475; William E. Borah, "The Reorganization of the Republican Party," *Vital Speeches*, I (Dec. 31, 1934), 202; William E. Borah, "Issues before the People," *Vital Speeches*, II (Apr. 6, 1936), 415; *NYT:* July 5, 1934, 13; July 25, 1934, 20; Nov. 13, 1935, 11.

10   *CR*, June 6, 1936, 9133-34, and Feb. 19, 1935, 2201, 2206-7.

11   Robert Lekachman, *The Age of Keynes* (New York, 1966), 139-40; *CR*, Feb. 4, 1936, 1433-34.

12   William E. Leuchtenburg, *Franklin D. Roosevelt and the New Deal* (New York, 1963), 246, 246 note 49.

13   *CR:* May 27, 1938, 7607-8; June 8, 1938, 8498; June 11, 1938, A 2591; June 16, 1938, A 2889; *NYT*, Jan. 28, 1938, 5; *CR*, May 23, 1938, 7255. Other New Dealers invoking the concept included Hopkins, Voorhis, Sherman Minton, and Theodore Francis Green.

14   *CR*, May 23, 1938, 7252.

15   Jackson, "The Philosophy of Big Business," *Vital Speeches*, 209-11; Jackson, "Should the Antitrust Laws Be Revised?" *United States Law Review*, 578-79, Testimony of Jackson, "Nomination of Robert H. Jackson," 109-10; *NYT:* Sept. 18, 1937, 30; Dec. 12, 1937, 5; Jan. 7, 1938, 6; Feb. 13, 1938, VIII, 4; *CR:* Nov. 17, 1937, A 63; Dec. 13, 1937, A 420-21; Jan. 5, 1938, A 33.

16   *CR*, May 23, 1938, 7248, and May 25, 1938, 7475; J. Joseph Huthmacher, *Senator Robert F. Wagner and the Rise of Urban Liberalism* (New York, 1968), 246, 246 note 27.

17   Lester G. Seligman and Elmer E. Cornwell, Jr., eds., *New Deal Mosaic: Roosevelt Confers with his National Emergency Council, 1933–1936* (Eugene, Ore., 1965), 387; Hawley, *New Deal and Monopoly*, 384, 467; Franklin D. Roosevelt, *The Public Papers and Addresses of Franklin D. Roosevelt (Public Papers)*, Samuel I. Rosenman, comp. (New York, 1938–50): III, 56; VI, 436, 529; VII, 63-64, 105-7, 306, 310-11; Franklin D. Roosevelt, Press Conferences (PC): Apr. 2, 1937, 6; Nov. 23, 1937, 23; Jan. 21, 1938, 9-10.

18   Roosevelt, PC, Apr. 2, 1937, 8; Roosevelt, *Public Papers*, VII, 338. This was a problem of long standing in FDR's mind. Rex Tugwell recalls of candidate Roosevelt: "He went on to express doubt that my alternative to inflation—the forcing down of selected prices so that a balance was

achieved—was practical. How could it be done? . . . How could prices be regulated? . . . He just could not visualize any device or mechanism . . . that could do these things—not in our system" (Rexford G. Tugwell, *The Brains Trust* [New York, 1968], 56-57).

19 Norman Thomas, "At the Front," *Socialist Call,* Mar. 27, 1937, 12.

20 Jackson, "The Philosophy of Big Business," *Vital Speeches,* 209.

21 *CR,* Nov. 17, 1937, 89.

22 Norman Beasley, *Frank Knox American* (New York, 1936), 156; George Henry Lobdell, Jr., "A Biography of Frank Knox" (Ph.D. thesis, University of Illinois, 1954), 258, 293; Frank Knox, *"We Planned It That Way"* (New York, 1938), 65, 67; Frank Knox, "A Policy of Abundance," *Vital Speeches,* I (July 1, 1935), 640; Frank Knox, "The Testing of the American Ideal," *Vital Speeches,* I (Aug. 26, 1935), 748-49; Frank Knox, *Labor under Dictatorships and Democracies* (Chicago, 1937), 7-9.

23 Donald R. McCoy, *Landon of Kansas* (Lincoln, Neb., 1966). 223, 404; Arthur M. Schlesinger, Jr., *The Age of Roosevelt: The Politics of Upheaval* (Boston, 1960), 611.

24 Herbert Hoover, *The Challenge to Liberty* (New York, 1935), 124-25; Herbert Hoover, *America's Way Forward* (New York, n.d.), 16, 24, 39, 41; Herbert Hoover, *The Memoirs of Herbert Hoover: The Great Depression, 1929–1941* (New York, 1952), 329, 351, 354; Herbert Hoover, *Addresses upon the American Road 1933–1938* (New York, 1938), 132, 136, 147-48, 154, 158, 160, 164, 170, 265, 315-16, 332, 351.

25 *NYT,* June 18, 1933, IV, 4; Ogden L. Mills, *Liberalism Fights On* (New York, 1936), 5-6, 8, 22, 26, 30, 67; Ogden L. Mills, *What of Tomorrow?* (New York, 1935), 2, 11, 69, 77, 83-85.

26 Lewis W. Douglas, *The Liberal Tradition* (New York, 1935), 55, 101; Lewis W. Douglas, "Government Fiscal Policies," *The Bankers Magazine,* CXXXI (July 1935), 77-78; Lewis W. Douglas, "A Federal Fiscal Policy Conducive to Recovery," *The Consensus,* XIX (Jan. 1935), 14; Lewis W. Douglas, "Balancing the National Budget," *The Consensus,* XXII (Jan. 1938), 15-16. Others denouncing the New Deal's "regimentation" included Democrats Joseph Ely, Bainbridge Colby, Thomas Gore, Al Smith, and James Reed, and Republicans Dickinson, Patterson, Snell, Wadsworth, Lowden, Christianson, Hatfield, Halleck, Joe Martin, Arthur Robinson, and Thomas Schall.

27 *NYT,* June 3, 1936, 20.

28 Douglas, *Liberal Tradition,* 1, 3-4, 10-13; Lewis W. Douglas, "Recovery by Balanced Budget," *Review of Reviews,* XCI (Apr. 1935), 25; Douglas, "A Federal Fiscal Policy Conducive to Recovery," *The Consensus,* 9.

29 Arthur M. Schlesinger, Jr., *The Age of Roosevelt: The Crisis of the Old Order* (Boston, 1957), 416-17; George Wolfskill, *The Revolt of the Conservatives* (Boston, 1962), 15-16.

30 Schlesinger, *Crisis of the Old Order,* 284-85, 416; *NYT,* Sept. 18, 1935, 12; Albert C. Ritchie *The American Bar—The Trustee of American Institutions,* American Liberty League Document No. 48 (Washington [a speech of June 29, 1935]), 4.

31 Morton Keller, *In Defense of Yesterday: James M. Beck and the Politics of Conservatism 1861-1936* (New York, 1958), 12-13, 223, 238.

32 *NYT,* Feb. 13, 1936, 16, and July 31, 1936, 8; Frank Knox, "Self-Reliance," *Vital Speeches,* II (Aug. 15, 1936), 709.

33 *NYT,* Aug. 4, 1934, 12.

34 *CR,* May 9, 1934, 8369.

35 *CR,* July 15, 1935, 11136, and July 22, 1935, 11553.

36 Mills, *Liberalism,* 26, 111; Mills, *What of Tomorrow?,* 2, 30, 40, 85-86, 112, 116, 121-26, 129, 137.

37 Hoover, *Challenge to Liberty,* 17, 84, 158, 201; Hoover, *Addresses,*

249. Senators L. J. Dickinson, Henry Hatfield, and Robert Carey also advanced the "reactionary" New Deal theme.

38 Alfred M. Landon, *America at the Crossroads,* Richard B. Fowler, ed. (New York, 1936), 32.

39 Hoover, *Challenge to Liberty,* 42, 123-25, 149, 177-79; Hoover, *America's Way Forward,* 38; Hoover, *Addresses,* 40-43, 131-32, 182, 289, 294.

40 Douglas, *Liberal Tradition,* 106-7.

41 Mills, *Liberalism,* 1-2, 4, 9, 20-21, 26, 28-33, 36-37, 40, 44, 46, 104, 112, 114, 156; Mills, *What of Tomorrow?,* 1, 4, 69, 85-86, 110, 115, 127-32; Ogden L. Mills, *The Seventeen Million* (New York, 1937), 3-5, 7, 38, 41-44, 52-53.

42 Others included Dickinson, Taber, and Henry Fletcher.

43 Quoted in James T. Patterson, *Congressional Conservatism and the New Deal* (Lexington, Ky., 1967), 29.

44 Earl Browder, *What Is Communism?* (New York, 1936), 29; Earl Browder, *Communism in the United States* (New York, 1935), 117; Upton Sinclair, *I, Candidate for Governor: And How I Got Licked* (Pasadena, 1935), 184; Thomas R. Amlie, "The End of Capitalism," *Common Sense,* II (Oct. 1933), 8.

45 Others included Taft, Ely, and Lowden.

46 Douglas, *Liberal Tradition,* 32.

47 *CR,* May 23, 1938, 7255.

48 Roosevelt, *Public Papers,* V, 337.

49 Edgar Kemler, *The Deflation of American Ideals* (Washington, 1941), 32-33.

50 Cary Smith Henderson, "Congressman John Taber of Auburn: Politics and Federal Appropriations, 1923-1962" (Ph.D thesis, Duke University, 1964), 63; Samuel B. Hand, "Al Smith, Franklin Roosevelt, and the New Deal: Some Comments on Perspective," *The Historian,* XXVII (May 1965), 368, 381; Jordan A. Schwarz, "Al Smith in the Thirties," *New York History,* XLV (Oct. 1964), 327-28.

51 Schlesinger, *Crisis of the Old Order,* 246-47, 434.

52 Rexford G. Tugwell, *The Stricken Land* (Garden City, N.Y., 1947), ix, 680-81; R. G. Tugwell, "The Protagonists: Roosevelt and Hoover," *The Antioch Review,* XIII (Dec. 1953), 428-29, 431; R. G. Tugwell, "The Preparation of a President," *Western Political Quarterly,* I (June 1948), 150; Tugwell, *The Brains Trust,* xxi-xxii, 44, 270; Paul K. Conkin, *The New Deal* (New York, 1967), 1, 7, 11-14.

53 Tugwell, *The Brains Trust,* 270; Rexford G. Tugwell, *The Democratic Roosevelt* (Garden City, N.Y., 1957), 34.

54 Roosevelt, *Public Papers,* IV, 342; Roosevelt, PC, Dec. 10, 1937, 7.

55 Roosevelt, *Public Papers,* VII, 587.

56 *NYT,* Apr. 8, 1936, 6.

57 Quoted in Otis L. Graham, Jr., *An Encore for Reform* (New York, 1967), 49.

58 Hoover, *Addresses,* 182.

CHAPTER 7: THE RECOVERY DEBATE: AN APPRAISAL

1 John Chamberlain, *Farewell to Reform* (Chicago: Quadrangle Books, [orig. pub. 1932]), 304-5.

2 John Dewey, *Liberalism and Social Action* (New York: Capricorn, 1963 [orig. pub. 1935]), 54, 90.

3 Quoted in James MacGregor Burns, *Roosevelt: The Lion and the Fox* (New York, 1956), 179.

INDEX

Adams, Alva, 135, 137, 139
Administered prices. *See* Monopoly problem
Agricultural Adjustment Act and Administration (AAA), and early New Deal, 8; views of, 59, 62-70; and economic interdependence, 61
Aiken, George, 72
Allen, Robert G., on causes of 1937-38 recession, 51; and Industrial Expansion, 92; and confidence thesis, 136; and purchasing power thesis, 137
Americans for Democratic Action, 4
Amlie, Thomas, and economic maturity, 23; and historic subsidization, 30; on crop control, 64; on New Deal planning, 79; and Industrial Expansion, 92, 95; and either-or theme, 108; mentioned, 138
Antimonopolism. *See* Monopoly problem
Antiplanning concept, versions and implications of, 19, 121-22; and exports cure, 46, 49; and money cure, 47, 49; and farm policy, 60; and Philip La Follette, 91; and shorter work week, 94, 96
Artificial prosperity concept, versions and implications of, 18, 31, 33, 115, 122-24; and foreign economic policy, 44, 45, 46, 47; and public spending, 55, 56, 57, 58
Austin, Warren, on depression's origins, 28; and 1937-38 recession, 138; mentioned, 134, 135, 139, 141, 142
Ayers, Roy, 24

Bacon, Robert, 135, 138
Bailey, Josiah, on depression's origins, 28; on recovery's delay, 29; and confidence thesis, 36, 37; and public spending, 56, 139, 140; on farm policy, 60, 64, 66; and planning, 77; and increased production, 92; and either-or-theme, 108; on capitalism and freedom, 108; and 1937-38 recession, 138; mentioned, 139, 141, 142

Baker, Newton, 106, 134, 137
Balance concept, versions and implications of, 18, 120-21; and NRA-AAA relationship, 69
Bankhead, John, 137, 138, 140
Bankhead, William, 137
Barbour, W. Warren, 139
Barkley, Alben, and confidence thesis, 38; on causes of 1937-38 recession, 51; on AAA, 63; and administered prices, 101; and purchasing power thesis, 137; and export trade, 137; mentioned, 137, 138, 139
Barton, Bruce, 37
Beck, James, on depression's origins, 28; on recovery's delay, 29; critical of Hoover and New Deal, 106; on New Deal as reactionary, 106; and regimentation theme, 129; mentioned, 135
Benson, Elmer, and purchasing power thesis, 137; and public spending, 140; mentioned, 133, 139
Black, Hugo, and economic maturity, 22; and frontier thesis, 24; and overexpansion, 25; supports purchasing power thesis, 42; criticizes NIRA, 88; on shorter work week, 94
Boileau, Gerald, 24, 137
Bone, Homer, and confidence thesis, 136; and purchasing power thesis, 137; mentioned, 133, 139
Borah, William, and confidence thesis, 38; supports purchasing power thesis, 42; and monetary formulae, 49; and monopoly problem, 51, 98, 99-100, 101, 102, 103; on farm policy, 61, 63, 64, 65, 66, 68, 69, 70, 73, 74; criticizes NRA, 88; and National Incorporation, 93-94; mentioned, viii
Bridges, Styles, on causes of 1937-38 recession, 50, 51; and recovery's delay, 135; mentioned, 134, 135, 139
Brookings Institution, 95, 103
Browder, Earl, 108, 133
Bryan, Charles, 141
Burdick, Usher, on causes of 1937-38 recession, 53; and monetary formulae, 137; mentioned, 133, 141

149

150

INDEX

Burke, Edward, 135
Byrd, Harry, supports confidence thesis, 36; and public spending, 56, 139, 140; on legislating prosperity, 77–78; mentioned, 139, 141
Byrnes, James, view of public spending, 56; on recovery agencies, 77; mentioned, 137, 140
Byrns, Joseph, 140

Cannon, Clarence, 65, 138
Capitalism, concepts of, and political liberty, 12, 108, 111; and New Dealers, 16–17, 70, 102, 130; and either-or theme, 108, 111; and views of New Deal, 114–15, 119
Capper, Arthur, 141
Carey, Robert, 67, 147
Celler, Emanuel, 64
Childs, Marquis, 129
Christianson, Theodore, 139, 141, 142, 146
Clark, Bennett Champ, 44, 137
Colby, Bainbridge, 135, 139, 142, 146
Committee for Economic Development, 3
Competition. See Monopoly problem
Confidence thesis, and conservatives, 9; and public spending, 34, 55, 57–58; expressions of, 35–37, 38; criticisms of, 37–38, 39; and 1937–38 recession, 50–51, 53; implications of, 116–18
Conkin, Paul, 15
Connally, Tom, 72, 137, 138
Conservative Manifesto, 36, 51
Conservatives, and confidence thesis, viii, 9, 35, 36, 38, 116–18; differences among, viii, 9; ideological strictures of, ix–x, 111; and economic maturity, 25–26, 32–33, 112–13, 114, 115, 116; and origins of depression, 28, 118; and natural recovery, 28–29; and causes of 1937–38 recession, 50–51, 53; and public spending, 55, 56, 57–58; and planning, 75, 76, 81–82; and NIRA, 82; and NRA, 87, 90; on implications of New Deal, 105, 110; and economic "systems," 108–9, 111; and artificial prosperity, 122–23
Copeland, Royal, on causes of 1937–38 recession, 51; on legislating prosperity, 77–78; mentioned, 139, 140
Costigan, Edward, 137
Croly, Herbert, 76
Crop control. See Agricultural Adjustment Act and Administration
Crowther, Frank, 135, 138
Cutting, Bronson, and economic maturity, 21; on purchasing power thesis, 42, 137; criticizes NRA, 87

Davis, James J., and New Deal defeatism,

134; and public spending, 140; mentioned, 135, 138
Davis, John W., critical of planning, 77; denounces Hoover and New Deal, 106; and regimentation theme, 129; mentioned, 138, 139
Dewey, John, 130
Dickinson, L. J., and economic maturity, 26; and public spending, 55; critical of planning, 77, 78; and NRA, 143; alleges New Deal regimentation, 146; and reactionary New Deal theme, 147; mentioned, 135, 139, 141, 142, 147
Dies, Martin, 138, 141
Dingell, John, 31
Dirksen, Everett, on NRA and AAA, 69; and New Deal contradictions, 142; mentioned, 135, 138
Doughton, Robert, and export trade, 44; and public spending, 139; mentioned, 137, 140
Douglas, Lewis, and economic maturity, 26–27; supports confidence thesis, 36; and foreign economic policy, 45, 46, 137; critical of public spending, 56; criticizes planning, 79; denounces collectivism, 105; on New Era and New Deal, 106; on economic freedom, 107; on planned economy, 108; intellectual rigidity of, 109; and economic liberalism, 129; mentioned, 9, 137, 142

Earle, George, and economic maturity, 21–22; supports purchasing power thesis, 42; on causes of 1937–38 recession, 51–52; on NIRA, 83; and confidence thesis, 136; mentioned, 135, 139
Eaton, Charles, 37, 134
Eccles, Marriner, 57, 76
Economic interdependence concept, and farm policy, 60–61, 62, 65, 66, 69, 72
Economic maturity concept, expressions of, 20–23, 31–32; criticisms of, 21, 25–28, 32–33; implications of, 113–14, 115–16, 123–24
Ellender, Allen, 61, 137
Ely, Joseph, on depression's origins, 28; alleges New Deal regimentation, 146; mentioned, 135, 139, 147
Emergency rationale, versions and implications of, 18–19, 120; and public spending, 54–55, 56, 57, 58; and crop control, 62–63, 68; and recovery agencies, 77
Exports cure, support for, 10, 43–47
Ezekiel, Mordecai, 92, 95

Fess, Simeon, on recovery's pace, 29,

National Recovery Administration
(NRA), and early New Deal, 8; impact on farmers, 65–66, 69; views of,
75, 82–90
New Dealers, and purchasing power
thesis, viii, 8, 39–40, 42, 43, 118–19;
ideological strictures of, x, 9, 10, 11,
12, 14–17, 46, 47, 70, 75, 89–90,
103–4, 111, 126–31; and American
political tradition, 11; and economic
maturity, 21, 32, 112–13, 114; and
confidence thesis, 37–38, 39; and
causes of 1937–38 recession, 51, 54;
and public spending, 55, 56, 58; and
planning, 75, 80–81, 82; and NRA,
89; and wage-and-hour legislation,
96; and monopoly problem, 101, 103,
104; and antiplanning concept, 122
New Left, xii
Norbeck, Peter, 65
Norris, George, on farm policy, 65; and
confidence thesis, 136; and purchasing power thesis, 137; and public
spending, 139; mentioned, 139
Nye, Gerald, and monetary formulae,
49; on farm policy, 60; on NRA's
farm impact, 65; criticizes NRA, 88;
and purchasing power thesis, 137

O'Connell, Jerry, 140
Olson, Floyd, 17–18, 129, 137
O'Mahoney, Joseph, on National Incorporation, 94; on monopoly problem,
98, 99, 100–101; and purchasing
power thesis, 137

Patman, Wright, 48, 49, 53
Patten, Simon, 76
Patterson, Roscoe, on New Deal as reactionary, 106; critical of NRA, 143;
alleges New Deal regimentation, 146;
mentioned, 134, 135, 139, 142
Pepper, Claude, and overexpansion, 25;
and confidence thesis, 38; and purchasing power thesis, 137; mentioned, 138, 139
Pinchot, Amos, 110
Pittman, Key, 138
Planning, and farm policy, 66, 70; views
of, 75–82; and NRA, 88–89, 90; and
Industrial Expansion bill, 92–93,
95–96
Pope, James, on causes of 1937–38 recession, 51; defends crop control, 64,
66–67; and administered prices, 101;
and purchasing power thesis, 137; and
export trade, 137; mentioned, 137,
138, 140
Pragmatism, and New Dealers, 14–17,
126–31
Progressives, and purchasing power
thesis, viii, 39–40, 42, 118; differences

among, viii; ideological strictures of,
10, 100–101, 111, 130–31; and economic maturity, 21, 22, 32, 112–13,
114; and confidence thesis, 37–38, 39;
and monetary formulae, 49; and public spending, 55; and NIRA, 82; and
NRA, 90; and monopoly problem,
103
Public spending, and later New Deal, 8;
views of, 34, 54–58; and 1937–38 recession, 51–52, 54, 56–57, 58; implications of, 123; in post-1940 era, 124
Purchasing power thesis, and New Dealers, 8, 9, 10, 11, 16; and public spending, 34, 56, 57; expressions of, 39–43;
and 1937–38 recession, 53, 54; and
farm policy, 59, 68–69; and NRA, 75,
83, 87, 88, 89, 90; and wage-and-hour
legislation, 94, 96; and monopoly
problem, 98, 101, 102, 103–4; implications of, 117, 118–19

Radicals, and purchasing power thesis,
viii, 42, 118–19; and political liberty,
12; and economic maturity, 21, 23,
32, 112–13, 114–15; and 1937–38 recession, 53–54; and planning, 76, 81–
82; and economic "systems," 111
Rainey, Henry, 24, 140
Rankin, John, espouses money cure, 48;
on causes of 1937–38 recession, 52–
53; on NRA's farm impact, 65;
mentioned, 137
Rayburn, Sam, 137
Reed, Daniel, 135, 138
Reed, David, on depression's origins, 28;
on recovery's progress, 29; espouses
confidence thesis, 36; on farm policy,
67; critical of planning, 77; critical
of NRA, 143; mentioned, 134, 139,
140
Reed, James, 135, 139, 146
Regimentation theme, and economic
isolation, 45, 46; and farm policy,
66–67, 70; versions of, 129
Reynolds, Robert, 71
Rich, Robert, 36
Ritchie, Albert, 106, 135, 139, 142
Robinson, Arthur, 134, 139, 146
Robinson, Joan, 5
Robinson, Joseph, defends AAA, 61;
and export trade, 137; and public
spending, 139; mentioned, 137
Roosevelt, Franklin, on New Deal values,
11; and frontier thesis, 24; and overexpansion, 25; espouses purchasing
power thesis, 41; and export trade,
44–45; on causes of 1937–38 recession, 51, 52; and public spending, 58;
on farm policy, 63, 67, 70, 72; and
planning, 76, 77, 80; on NRA, 82–83,
86–87, 89; on wage-and-hour legisla-